Does the Birth Control Pill Cause Abortions?

by Randy Alcorn

8th edition, revised 2007
(1st edition was August 1997)

Eternal Perspective Ministries (EPM)
39085 Pioneer Blvd., Suite 206
Sandy, OR 97055
503-668-5200 · Fax: 503-668-5252
www.epm.org

Cost per book *(Add 10% shipping, 7% shipping for orders of 100 or more copies)*

1	$3.00
2-9	$2.50
10-99	$2.25
100-499	$2.00
500	$1.75

Endorsements by Physicians:

"Scientific papers suggest that escape ovulation occurs 4-15% of all cycles in patients taking birth control pills. Thus, as this booklet points out, early chemical abortions are a real and significant concern."
Paddy Jim Baggot, M.D., Ob/Gyn,
Fellow of the American College of Medical Genetics

"Randy Alcorn has thoroughly studied and written on an area where little published scientific information exists. His responses to this issue, and his outstanding appendices, are must reading."
William M. Petty, M.D., Surgeon,
Gynecologic Oncology

"Randy Alcorn has once again demonstrated his tenacity and integrity in pursuing the truth. He has exposed the abortifacient properties of so-called birth control agents. This booklet should be required reading for all discerning Christians who wish to fully live out their faith."
William L. Toffler, M.D.
Professor of Family Medicine, Oregon Health Sciences University

"Somehow the concerns about the abortifacient effects of the pill and other hormonal contraceptives never really bothered me. I am amazed now that I could have ignored this issue in the past. I've now discontinued prescribing hormonal contraception."
Stephen K. Toadvine, M.D.
Rush-Copley Family Practice, Aurora, IL

Other Books by Randy Alcorn

Fiction:

Deadline
Deception
Dominion
Edge of Eternity
The Ishbane Conspiracy (with daughters)
Lord Foulgrin's Letters
Safely Home
Tell Me About Heaven
Wait Until Then

Nonfiction:

50 Days of Heaven
The Grace & Truth Paradox
Heaven
Heaven for Kids
In Light of Eternity
Is Rescuing Right?
The Law of Rewards
Money, Possessions, and Eternity
Prolife Answers to Prochoice Arguments
The Purity Principle
Restoring Sexual Sanity
Sexual Temptation
The Treasure Principle
Why ProLife?
Women Under Stress

Table of Contents

Evidence to the Contrary?

How Often Does the Pill Cause Abortions?

Responding to the Evidence: Questions & Objections

Conclusion

Appendices

Introduction

What's at Stake Here?

"The Pill" is the popular term for more than forty different commercially available oral contraceptives. In medicine, they are commonly referred to as BCPs (Birth Control Pills), OCs (Oral Contraceptives) and/or OCPs (Oral Contraceptive Pills). They are also called "Combination Pills," because they contain a combination of estrogen and progestin.

About fourteen million American women use the Pill each year. Across the globe it is used by about sixty million. The question of whether it causes abortions has direct bearing on untold millions of Christians, many of them prolife, who use and recommend it. For those who recognize God is the Creator of each person and the giver and taker of human life, this is a question with profound moral implications. After coming to grips with the importance of this issue, and hearing conflicting opinions for the last few years, I determined to research this question thoroughly and communicate my findings, whether or not I liked what I found.

I wanted, and still want, the answer to this question to be "No." I came to this issue as a skeptic. Though I heard people here and there make an occasional claim that the Pill caused abortions, I learned long ago not to trust everything said by sincere Christians, who are sometimes long on zeal but short on careful research. While I'm certainly fallible, I have taken pains to be as certain as possible that the information I am presenting here is accurate. I've examined medical journals and other scientifically oriented sources—everything from popular medical reference books to highly technical professional periodicals. I've checked and double-checked, submitted this research to physicians, and asked clarifying questions of pharmacists and other experts. Few of my citations are from prolife advocates. Most are physicians, scientists, researchers, pill-manufacturers and other secular sources.

I am not a physician or a scientist, but I am an experienced researcher. If I were conducting medical research, obviously the fact that I am not a physician or scientist would disqualify me. But I have attempted no medical research. I have simply hunted down, read, and organized the research findings of others. I have then evaluated their cumulative findings and added my own insights in areas where I am more qualified, including biblical studies.

The first edition of this book came out in 1997. While I had to dig deep to find information on the subject back then, in the past few years there has been an explosion of relevant inquiry into it. According to Dr. John Wilks, a pharmacist, "new research appears almost monthly to illuminate further and sometimes confuse [the] emerging medical discipline associated with fertilization and implantation technology."[1]

Since it is critical that I cite credible medical and scientific sources, there is no way to avoid using medical terminology in this book. I have tried to minimize this by using only brief quotations and whenever possible avoiding technical terms.

This little book cannot be all things to all people. Its readers will include high school students, young married couples and medical lay people who want simple straightforward answers devoid of technical terms. It will also include physicians, pharmacists and research scientists, who would neither read, respect, nor benefit from a simplistic and sketchy presentation on such a significant issue.

Some readers want and need as much documentation and explanation as possible. Others are satisfied with one or two evidences for any claim. If the reader feels a point has been adequately made to him, he can simply skim or move on to the next heading that interests him. Meanwhile, those who desire to work through the details can do so. Those who desire a less detailed version of this book can go to Appendix E in the new expanded and revised version of my book *ProLife Answers to ProChoice Arguments* (Multnomah Publishers, 2000). Dr. Walt Larimore and I co-authored a different and even more abbreviated presentation that appears as a chapter in *The Reproduction Revolution*.[2] The book in your hands is the most thorough and best-documented presentation of my conclusions on this subject matter.

Before going further, let me affirm a truth that is a foundational premise of all I am about to address: ***God creates each human being at the point of conception***.* This is the clear teaching of the Bible and is confirmed by the scientific evidence. If you are not *completely* convinced of this, please stop now and read the first two appendices. They both answer the question, "When Does Human Life Begin?" Appendix A gives the answer of Scripture and appendix B the answer of science. You may also wish to read the other appendices to bring a biblical perspective to the importance of the issue dealt with in this book.

Because there is so much at stake, and because there is a great spiritual battle surrounding this issue, I suggest readers pause and pray, asking God to show you his mind and his heart.

What is a Contraceptive?

Conception is the point at which the twenty-three chromosomes from the female's egg and the twenty-three from the male's sperm join together to form a new human life, with forty-six chromosomes and his or her own distinct DNA.

Often the newly conceived person is referred to as a "fertilized egg." This term is dehumanizing and misleading. Neither egg (ovum) nor sperm alone is in any sense a human being, but merely the product of a human being. However, at the point of fertilization someone brand new comes into existence, a singularly unique human being. As the sperm no longer exists, neither in essence does the egg. It is replaced by a new creation with unique DNA, rapidly growing and dividing on its own. This new human being is no more a mere "fertilized egg" than it is a "modified sperm." He is a newly created person, with the equivalent of hundreds of volumes of distinct genetic programming.

Historically, the terms conception and fertilization have been virtually synonymous, both referring to the very beginning of human life. A contraceptive, then, just as it sounds, was something that prevented fertilization (i.e. *contra*dicted *concep*tion). Unfortunately, in the last few decades alternative meanings of "conception" and "contraception" have emerged, which have greatly confused the issue.

Eugene F. Diamond, M.D., wrote an excellent article in Focus on the Family's *Physician* magazine. Dr. Diamond states,

> Prior to 1976, a "contraceptive" was understood to be an agent that prevented the union of sperm and ovum. In 1976 the American College of Obstetricians and Gynecologists (ACOG), realizing that this definition didn't help its political agenda, arbitrarily changed the definition.
>
> A contraceptive now meant anything that prevented implantation of the blastocyst, which occurs six or seven days after fertilization. Conception, as defined by *Dorland's Illustrated Medical Dictionary* (27th Edition), became "the onset of pregnancy marked by implantation of the blastocyst."
>
> The hidden agenda in ACOG's redefinition of "contraceptive" was to blur the distinction between agents preventing fertilization and those preventing implantation of the week-old embryo. Specifically, abortifacients such as IUDs, combination pills, minipills, progestin-only pills, injectables such as Provera and, more recently, implantables such as Norplant, all are contraceptives by this definition.[3]

(Note that Dr. Diamond identifies combination pills, collectively known as "the Pill," as abortifacients. Whether or not he is correct is what this book is about.)

The redefinition of "contraceptive" Dr. Diamond speaks of has gradually crept into the medical literature. Because of the change, some medical professionals will state the Pill is only a contraceptive, even if they know it sometimes acts to prevent implantation. But the old meaning of contraceptive, the one more scientifically accurate and distinct, is also still widely used.

I have in front of me a recently issued metallic circular "Pregnancy Calculator," produced by Wyeth-Ayerst Laboratories, a leading manufacturer of the Pill. These are routinely used by Ob/GYNs to calculate a pregnant woman's due date. The calculator points to the first day of the last menstrual period, then points to 14-15 days later as "Probable Day of Conception." However, implantation (also called nidation) does not happen until day 21 of the new cycle, six or seven days after conception. Hence, the Pill-manufacturer that makes the pregnancy calculator still defines "conception" in its historical sense, not that adopted by the ACOG.

According to the meaning conception always had—which is the meaning still held to by the vast majority of the public and many if not most medical professionals—there is no way any product is acting as a contraceptive when it prevents implantation. (Call it a contra-*implantive*, if you wish, but when it works in that way it is not a contraceptive.)

In this book, I will use "conception" in its classic sense—as a synonym for fertilization, the point at which the new human life begins. Contraceptives, then, are chemicals or devices that prevent conception or fertilization. A birth control method that sometimes kills an already conceived human being is *not* merely a contraceptive. It may function as a contraceptive some or most of the time, but some of the time it is also an abortifacient.

15

The problem of "contraceptives" that are really abortifacients is not a new one. Many prolife Christians, including physicians, have long opposed the use of Intra-Uterine Devices (IUDs), as well as RU-486 ("the abortion pill") and the Emergency Contraceptive Pill (ECP). Some, though not all, have also opposed Norplant, Depo-Provera, and the "Mini-pill," all of which sometimes or often fail to prevent conception, but succeed in preventing implantation of the six day old human being. (For more details, see "The IUD, Norplant, Depo-Provera, RU-486, and the Mini-Pill," in the addendum following the appendices.)

But what about the widely used Birth Control Pill, with its combined estrogen and progestin. Is it exclusively a contraceptive? That is, does it always prevent conception? Or does it, like other products, sometimes prevent implantation, thus producing an early abortion? That is the central question of this book.

My Own Vested Interest in the Pill

To make the issue personal, let me tell you my own story. In 1991, while researching my book *ProLife Answers to ProChoice Arguments*, I heard someone suggest that birth control pills can cause abortions. This was brand new to me—in all my years as a pastor and a prolifer, I had never heard it before. I was immediately skeptical.

My vested interests were strong in that Nanci and I used the Pill in the early years of our marriage, as did many of our prolife friends. Why not? We believed it simply prevented conception. We never suspected it had any potential for abortion. No one told us this was

16

even a possibility. I confess I never read the fine print of the Pill's package insert, nor am I sure I would have understood it even if I had.

In fourteen years as a pastor, doing considerable premarital counseling, I always warned couples against the IUD because I'd read it causes early abortions. I typically recommended young couples use the Pill because of its relative ease and effectiveness.

At the time I was researching *ProLife Answers*, I found only one person who could point me toward any documentation that connected the Pill and abortion. She told me of just one primary source that supported this belief and I came up with only one other. Still, these two sources were sufficient to compel me to include this warning in my book:

> Some forms of contraception, specifically the intrauterine device (IUD), Norplant, and certain low-dose oral contraceptives, often do not prevent conception but prevent implantation of an already fertilized ovum. The result is an early abortion, the killing of an already conceived individual. Tragically, many women are not told this by their physicians, and therefore do not make an informed choice about which contraceptive to use…Among prolifers there is honest debate about contraceptive use and the degree to which people should strive to control the size of their families. But on the matter of controlling family size by killing a family member, we all ought to agree. Solutions based on killing people are not viable.[4]

At the time, I incorrectly believed that "low-dose" birth control pills were the exception, not the rule. I thought most people who took the Pill were in no danger of having abortions. What I've found in my recent research is that **since 1988 virtually *all* oral contraceptives used in America are low-dose, that is, they contain much lower levels of estrogen than the earlier birth control pills**.

The standard amount of estrogen in the birth control pills of the 1960's and early 70's was 150 micrograms. *Danforth's Obstetrics and Gynecology*[5] says this:

> The use of estrogen-containing formulations with less than 50 micrograms of estrogen steadily increased to 75% of all prescriptions in the United States in 1987. In the same year, only 3% of the prescriptions were for formulations that contained more than 50 micrograms of estrogen. Because these higher-dose estrogen formulations have a greater incidence of adverse effects without greater efficacy, they are no longer marketed in the United States.

After the Pill had been on the market fifteen years, many serious negative side effects of estrogen had been clearly proven.[6] These included blurred vision, nausea, cramping, irregular menstrual bleeding, migraine headaches and increased incidence of breast cancer, strokes and heart attacks, some of which led to fatalities.

Beginning in the mid-seventies, manufacturers of the Pill steadily decreased the content of estrogen and progestin in their products. The average dosage of estrogen in the Pill declined from 150 micrograms in 1960 to 35 micrograms in 1988. The Association of Reproductive Health Professionals and Ortho Pharmaceutical Corporation directly state these facts in their own advertisement.[7]

Likewise, Pharmacists for Life confirms:

> As of October 1988, the newer lower dosage birth
> control pills are the only type available in the U.S., by
> mutual agreement of the Food and Drug
> Administration and the three major Pill manufacturers:
> Ortho, Searle and Syntex.[8]

What is now considered a "high dose" of estrogen is
50 micrograms, which is in fact a very low dose in
comparison to the 150 micrograms once standard for
the Pill. The "low-dose" pills of today are mostly 20-35
micrograms. As far as I can tell from looking them up
individually in medical reference books, there are no
birth control pills available today that have more than
50 micrograms of estrogen. An M.D. wrote to inform
me that she too made a similar search and could find
none. If they exist, they are certainly rare.

Not only was I wrong in thinking low-dose
contraceptives were the exception rather than the
rule, I didn't realize there was considerable
documented medical information linking birth control
pills and abortion. The evidence was there, I just
didn't probe deep enough to find it. More evidence
has surfaced in the years since.

I say all this to emphasize I came to this research with
no prejudice against the Pill. In fact, I came with a
prejudice *toward* it. I certainly don't want to believe I
may have jeopardized the lives of my own newly
conceived children, nor that I was wrong in
recommending it to all those couples I counseled as a
pastor. It would take compelling evidence for me to
overcome the reluctance I brought to this, and to
change my position.

Still, I resolved to pursue this research with an open mind, sincerely seeking the truth and hoping to find out the Pill does not cause abortions. I ask you to take a look with me at the evidence and decide for yourself.

A warning is in order, since many readers come to this issue with vested interests on one of two sides. Those who oppose contraceptives per se may be biased toward the notion that the Pill causes abortions. Since they are against the Pill anyway, believing that it causes abortions gives them one more reason, perhaps the best reason of all, to oppose it. Hence, they may tend to accept uncritically any arguments against the Pill.

Likewise, readers who have used the Pill or recommended it and Christian physicians who prescribe and make a significant amount of income from the Pill—including most OB-GYNs and family practitioners—will naturally have vested interests in believing the Pill does not cause abortions.

Those coming with either bias should resist the temptation to believe something about the Pill simply because they want to. Hard as it may be, let's attempt to evaluate the evidence fairly and objectively.

Examining the Evidence

The Physician's Desk Reference (PDR)

The *Physician's Desk Reference* is the most frequently used reference book by physicians in America. The *PDR*, as it's often called, lists and explains the effects, benefits and risks of every medical product that can legally be prescribed. The Food and Drug Administration requires that each manufacturer provide accurate information on its products, based on scientific research and laboratory tests. This information is included in The *PDR*.

As you read the following, keep in mind that the term "implantation," by definition, *always* involves an already conceived human being. Therefore any agent that serves to prevent implantation functions as an abortifacient.

This is *PDR's* product information for Ortho-Cept, as listed by Ortho, one of the largest manufacturers of the Pill:

> Combination oral contraceptives act by suppression of gonadotropins. Although the primary mechanism of this action is inhibition of ovulation, other alterations include changes in the cervical mucus, which increase the difficulty of sperm entry into the uterus, and **changes in the endometrium, which reduce the likellhood of implantation.**[9]

The FDA-required research information on the birth control pills Ortho-Cyclen and Ortho Tri-Cyclen also state that they cause "**changes in...the endometrium (which reduce the likelihood of implantation).**"[10]

Notice that these changes in the endometrium, and their reduction in the likelihood of implantation, are not stated by the manufacturer as speculative or theoretical effects, but as actual ones. (The importance of this will surface later in the book.)

Similarly, Syntex, another major pill-manufacturer, says this in the *Physician's Desk Reference* under the "Clinical Pharmacology" of the six pills it produces (two types of Brevicon and four of Norinyl):

Although the primary mechanism of this action is inhibition of ovulation, other alterations include **changes in** the cervical mucus (which increase the difficulty of sperm entry into the uterus), and **the endometrium (which may reduce the likelihood of implantation).**[11]

Wyeth says something very similar of its combination Pills, including Lo/Ovral and Ovral: "other alterations include**...changes in the endometrium which reduce the likelihood of implantation.**"[12] Wyeth makes virtually identical statements about its birth control pills Nordette[13] and Triphasil.[14]

A young couple showed me their pill, Desogen, a product of Organon. I looked it up in the *PDR*. It states one effect of the pill is to create "**changes in the endometrium which reduce the likelihood of implantation.**"[15]

The inserts packaged with birth control pills are condensed versions of longer research papers detailing the Pill's effects, mechanisms and risks. Near the end, the insert typically says something like the following, which is directly from the Desogen pill insert:

> If you want more information about birth control pills, ask your doctor, clinic or pharmacist. They have a more technical leaflet called the Professional Labeling, which you may wish to read. The Professional Labeling is also published in a book entitled *Physician's Desk Reference*, available in many bookstores and public libraries.

Of the half dozen birth control pill package inserts I've read, only *one* included the information about the Pill's abortive mechanism. This was a package insert dated July 12, 1994, found in the oral contraceptive Demulen, manufactured by Searle.[16] Yet **this abortive mechanism was *referred to in all cases* in the FDA-required manufacturer's Professional Labeling**, as documented in the *Physician's Desk Reference*.

In summary, according to multiple references throughout the *Physician's Desk Reference*, which articulate the research findings of all the birth control pill manufacturers, there are **not one but three mechanisms of birth control pills:** 1) inhibiting ovulation (the primary mechanism), 2) thickening the cervical mucus, thereby making it more difficult for sperm to travel to the egg, and 3) thinning and shriveling the lining of the uterus to the point that it is unable or less able to facilitate the implantation of the newly-fertilized egg. **The first two mechanisms are contraceptive. The third is abortive.**

Naturally, compliance by the patient in regularly taking the Pill is a huge factor in its rate of suppressing ovulation. But, as we will see later in this book, breakthrough ovulation happens even among those who never miss a pill.

When a woman taking the Pill discovers she is pregnant—according to the *Physician's Desk Reference*'s efficacy rate tables, listed under every contraceptive, this is 3% of pill-takers *each year*—it means that **all three of these mechanisms have failed**. The third mechanism *sometimes* fails in its role as backup, just as the first and second mechanisms sometimes fail. However, each and every time the third mechanism succeeds, it causes an abortion.

Dr. Walter Larimore and I co-authored a chapter in *The Reproduction Revolution*, presenting evidence that the birth control pill can, in fact, cause abortions.[17] Dr. Susan Crockett and four colleagues presented the opposing view.[18] Dr. Crockett believes any abortifacient effect is so minimal as to be unworthy of concern. She discounts the repeated *PDR* references to adverse endometrial changes that sometimes prevent implantation, saying, "Hormone contraceptive literature is written for marketing purposes ('this contraception will prevent pregnancy') and for legal protection ('you can't sue if you miscarry—we warned you'), as well as for patient education."[19]

Proponents of the view that there is an abortifacient effect (including the author) counter that the disclosure of such information is mandated by no less an authority than the FDA. While such information may serve a legal purpose, its inclusion is clearly more than a marketing ploy or a legal caveat. Those who believe that the manufacturers' claims *that the Pill sometimes prevents implantation* are not accurate statements—that they are not truths based on science, but falsehoods motivated by public relations—have the responsibility to address both the companies and the FDA with this serious accusation. They should not, however, expect consumers to simply disregard them in favor of a more desirable belief.[20]

Dr. Brian Clowes, a researcher with Human Life International, points out that stated *PDR* failure rates don't tell the whole story:

> These failure rates are indicative only of the number of human embryos that reach the stage of a verifiable implanted pregnancy [sustained pregnancy]; no indication is given of the scale of loss of human embryos that fail to implant at the endometrial level under the hormonal influence of these drugs. This occurrence essentially amounts to early chemical abortion.[21]

Medical Journals and Textbooks

The Pill alters what are known as epithelial and stromal integrins, which appear to be related to endometrial receptivity, i.e., the ability of the endometrium to cooperate with the embryo in implantation. These integrins are considered markers of normal fertility. Significantly, they are conspicuously absent in patients with various conditions associated with infertility *and* in women taking the Pill. Since normal implantation involves a precise synchronization of the zygote's development with the endometrial window of maximum receptivity, the

25

absence of these integrins logically indicates a higher failure rate of implantation for Pill-takers. According to Dr. Stephen G. Somkuti and his research colleagues,

> These data suggest that the morphological changes observed in the endometrium of OC users have functional significance and provide evidence that **reduced endometrial receptivity does indeed contribute to the contraceptive efficacy of OCs.**[22]

Shoham and his research associates reported findings in a *Fertility & Sterility* journal article. Their studies indicate a "mid-luteal endometrial thickness of 11 mm or more…was found to be a good prognostic factor for detecting early [sustained] pregnancy," and no [sustained] pregnancies could be identified "when the endometrial thickness was less than 7 mm."[23]

Drs. Chowdhury, Joshi and associates state,

> The data suggests that though missing of the low dose combination pills may result in 'escape' ovulation in some women, however, the **pharmacological effects of pills on the endometrium** and cervical mucus **may continue to provide them contraceptive protection**."[24]

(Note in both the proceeding and following citations "contraceptive" is used in the sense it was redefined by the ACOG, so it now includes the endometrium's diminished capacity to accept implantation of the already conceived child.)

In a study of oral contraceptives published in a major medical journal, Dr. G. Virginia Upton, Regional Director of Clinical Research for Wyeth, one of the major birth control pill manufacturers, says this:

The graded increments in LNg in the triphasic OC serve to maximize contraceptive protection by increasing the viscosity of the cervical mucus (cervical barrier), by suppressing ovarian progesterone output, and **by causing endometrial changes that will not support implantation**.[25]

Dr. Goldzieher says as a result of the combined Pill's action, "possibly the endometrium in such cycles may provide additional contraceptive protection."[26]

The medical textbook *Williams Obstetrics* states, "progestins **produce an endometrium that is unfavorable to blastocyst implantation**."[27]

Drs. Ulstein and Myklebust of the University of Bergen, Norway state,

> The main effect of oral contraception is inhibition of ovulation. Furthermore the **changes in** the cervical mucus and **the endometrium are considered to be of importance to contraceptive effectiveness**.[28]

Drug Facts and Comparisons says this about birth control pills in its 1996 edition:

> Combination OCs inhibit ovulation by suppressing the gonadotropins, follicle-stimulating hormone (FSH) and lutenizing hormone (LH). Additionally, **alterations in** the genital tract, including cervical mucus (which inhibits sperm penetration) and **the endometrium (which reduces the likelihood of implantation**), may contribute to contraceptive effectiveness.[29]

A standard medical reference, *Danforth's Obstetrics and Gynecology*[30] states this: "The production of glycogen by the endometrial glands is diminished by the ingestion of oral contraceptives, **which impairs the survival of the blastocyst in the uterine cavity**." (The blastocyst is the newly conceived child.)

It is well documented that the cellular structure of the endometrium is altered by the Pill, producing areas of edema alternating with areas of dense cellularity, which constitute an abnormal state not conducive to a pregnancy.[31]

Magnetic Resonance Imaging studies demonstrate that the lining of the endometrium is dramatically thinned in Pill users. Normal endometrial thickness that can sustain a pregnancy ranges in density from 5 to 13 mm. The average thickness in pill users is 1.1 mm.[32][33]

Sherrill Sellman describes the Pill's effects as follows:

...[causing] alterations to the lining of the womb, converting the proliferative nature of the endometrium—which is naturally designed to accept and sustain a fertilized ovum—to a secretory endometrium, which is a thin, devasculating lining, **physiologically unreceptive to receiving and sustaining a zygote**.[34]

In her article "Abortifacient Drugs and Devices: Medical and Moral Dilemmas," Dr. Kristine Severyn states,

The third effect of combined oral contraceptives is to **alter the endometrium in such a way that implantation of the fertilized egg (new life) is made more difficult, if not impossible**. In effect, **the endometrium becomes atrophic and unable to support implantation of the fertilized egg**...the alteration of the endometrium, making it **hostile to implantation** by the fertilized egg, provides **a backup abortifacient method** to prevent pregnancy.[35]

A 1999 Guttmacher Institute publication includes the following statement concerning the "Emergency Contraceptive Pill" (ECP):

> The best scientific evidence suggests that ECP's most often work by suppressing ovulation. But depending on the timing of intercourse in relation to a woman's hormonal cycle, **they—as is the case with *all* hormonal contraceptive methods—also may prevent pregnancy** either by preventing fertilization or **by preventing implantation of a fertilized egg in the uterus**.[36]

Note what isn't said directly, but which is nonetheless indicated for all who have eyes to see—one primary way this product works is by causing the death of an already conceived child. These technical terms go unexamined by most readers, including physicians. It is only when you stop and think about the significance of preventing implantation that you come to terms with what it really means. Most people, including most prolife Christians, simply don't stop and think. It's significant to note that while ECPs may be more efficient in preventing implantation than the Pill, their stated means of operation are actually the same.

What Does All this Mean?

Contraceptive Technology, dealing with the impact of OCPs on a woman's endometrium, states, "secretions within the uterus are altered as is the cellular structure of the endometrium leading to the production of areas of edema alternating with areas of dense cellularity."[37]

As a woman's menstrual cycle progresses, her endometrium gradually gets richer and thicker in preparation for the arrival of any newly conceived child who may be there to attempt implantation. In a natural cycle, unimpeded by the Pill, the endometrium produces an increase in blood vessels, which allow a greater blood supply to bring oxygen and nutrients to the child. There is also an increase in the endometrial stores of glycogen, a sugar that serves as a food source for the blastocyst (child) as soon as he or she implants.

The Pill keeps the woman's body from creating the most hospitable environment for a child, resulting instead in an endometrium that is deficient in both food (glycogen) and oxygen. The child may die because he lacks this nutrition and oxygen.

Cell-signaling, communications between Integrins in the womb and surrounding the traveling egg, are disrupted and hamper healthy implanting of the embryo into the endometrium. In a 1997 medical journal, this effect on the endometrium is portrayed in a graphic analogy:

> Consider the example of a space shuttle, low on fuel and oxygen, urgently needing to dock with the space station. The mother ship and the shuttle communicate with each other so that the shuttle knows which docking bay to go to. Importantly, the mother ship knows which bay to make ready. Successful communication is imperative. If this electronic communication fails (disrupted embryo-uterine 'cell-talk') the shuttle may go to the wrong docking bay, fail to attach to the mother ship, drift away, with the result that the crew dies from a lack

of food and oxygen. Alternately, the shuttle might go to the right bay but find that all the docking apparatus is not in place. Again, the attachment between the two fails due to faulty communication and the crew dies…. To continue the analogy, the Integrins could be thought of as grappling hooks that 'hold' the human embryo onto the womb whilst the process of implantation is completed.[38]

Typically, the new person attempts to implant at six days after conception. If implantation is unsuccessful, the child is flushed out of the womb in a miscarriage that may appear to be nothing more than a normal, even if delayed, menstruation. While there are many spontaneous miscarriages, whenever the miscarriage is the result of an environment created by a foreign device or chemical, it is an artificially induced miscarriage, which is, in fact, an abortion. This is true even if the mother does not intend it, is not aware of it happening, and would be horrified if she knew.

If the embryo is still viable when it reaches the uterus, **underdevelopment of the uterine lining caused by the Pill prevents implantation**. The embryo dies and the remains are passed along in the next bleeding episode, which, incidentally, is not a true menstruation, even though it is usually perceived as such.[39]

Research Findings
Back to the 1970's

One of the things that surprised me in my research was that though many recent sources testify to the Pill's abortive capacity, it has actually been well established for three decades. In 1966 Dr. Alan

Guttmacher, former director of Planned Parenthood, said this about the Pill's effect on the uterine lining:

> The appearance of the endometrium differs so markedly from a normal premenstrual endometrium that one doubts it could support implantation of a fertilized egg.[40]

The following nine sources are all from the 1970s. (Keep in mind that the term "blastocyst" refers to the newly conceived human being—"it" is not a thing, but a person, a "he" or "she.")

Dr. Daniel R. Mishell of the USC School of Medicine said,

> Furthermore, [the combination pills] **alter the endometrium** so that glandular production of glycogen is diminished and **less energy is available for the blastocyst to survive** in the uterine cavity.[41]

Dr. J. Richard Crout, president of the Food and Drug Administration (FDA), said this of combination birth control pills:

> Fundamentally, these pills take over the menstrual cycle from the normal endocrine mechanisms. And in so doing they inhibit ovulation and **change the characteristics of the uterus so that it is not receptive to a fertilized egg.**[42]

In 1970, J. Peel and M. Potts's *Textbook of Contraceptive Practice* acknowledged this:

> In addition to its action on the pituitary-ovarian axis the combination products [BCPs] also alter the character of the cervical mucus, modify the tubal

transport of the egg and **may have an effect on the endometrium to make implantation unlikely**.[43]

In their book *Ovulation in the Human*, P. G. Crosignani and D. R. Mishell stated that birth control pills **"affect the endometrium, reducing glycogen production by the endometrial glands which is necessary to support the blastocyst**."[44]

The *Handbook of Obstetrics & Gynecology*, then a standard reference work, states,

> The combination pill…is effective because LH release is blocked and ovulation does not occur; tubal motility is altered and fertilization is impeded; **endometrial maturation is modified so that implantation is unlikely**; and cervical mucus is thickened and sperm migration blocked.[45]

Note that in this case *four* mechanisms are mentioned, including tubal motility, which we will address later. Note also that prevention of implantation is listed before the prevention of conception by the thickened cervical mucus.

In 1979 a spokesperson for Ortho Pharmaceutical Corporation, stated,

> The lining of the uterus does not become fully developed so that even if an egg does ripen and is fertilized, there is little likelihood that it would become implanted.[46]

It was not just obscure medical journals and textbooks that contained this information in the 70's. The popular magazine *Changing Times* explained, "The pill may affect the movement of the fertilized egg toward the uterus or **prevent it from imbedding**

itself in the uterine lining."[47] Likewise, the book *My Body, My Health* stated,

> In a natural cycle, the uterine lining thickens under the influence of estrogen during the first part of the cycle, and then matures under the influence of both progesterone and estrogen after ovulation. This development sequence is not possible during a Pill cycle because both progestin and estrogen are present throughout the cycle. **Even if ovulation and conception did occur, successful implantation would be unlikely.**[48]

Proabortionists Know: Why Don't We?

If most prolifers have been slow to catch on to this established medical knowledge (I certainly have been), many proabortionists are fully aware of it. In February 1992, writing in opposition to a Louisiana law banning abortion, Tulane Law School Professor Ruth Colker wrote,

> Because **nearly all birth control devices, except the diaphragm and condom, operate between the time of conception...and implantation**...the statute would appear to ban most contraceptives.[49]

Colker referred to all those methods, including the Pill, which sometimes prevent implantation.

Similarly, attorney Frank Sussman, representing Missouri Abortion Clinics, argued before the Supreme Court in 1989 that "The most common forms of...contraception today, **IUDs and low-dose birth control pills...act as abortifacients.**"[50]

Remember, by that time all Pills were "low-dose" compared to the Pill of the 60's and 70's. In fact, 97% were low-dose even by recent standards, in that they had less than fifty micrograms of estrogen.

The Pill's ability to prevent implantation is such well-established knowledge that the 1982 edition of the *Random House College Dictionary*, on page 137, actually defines "Birth Control Pill" as "an oral contraceptive for women that **inhibits ovulation, fertilization, or implantation of a fertilized ovum**, causing temporary infertility." (I'm not suggesting, of course, that *Random House* or any dictionary is an authoritative source. My point is that the knowledge of the Pill's prevention of implantation is so firmly established that it can be presented as standard information in a household reference book. That this is unknown to and denied by so many Christians is remarkable to say the least.)

I found on the World Wide Web a number of sources that recognize the abortive mechanism of the Pill. (Again, web sources are not authoritative—my point is to demonstrate a widespread awareness of the Pill's abortive properties.) For instance, "Oral Contraceptives: Frequently Asked Questions," says, "The combined oral contraceptive pill…**impedes Implantation of an egg into the endometrium (uterine lining) because it changes that lining.**"[51]

For years proabortionists have argued that if the Human Life Amendment, which recognizes each human life begins at conception, was to be put into law, this would lead to the banning of both the IUD and the Pill. When hearing this I used to think, "They're misrepresenting the facts and agitating people by pretending the Pill would be jeopardized by the HLA."

I realize now that while their point *was* to agitate people against the Human Life Amendment, they were actually correct in saying that if the amendment was passed and taken seriously, the Pill's legality would be jeopardized. They never claimed the Human Life Amendment would make condoms or diaphragms illegal. Why? Because when they work, those methods are 100% contraceptives—they *never* cause abortions. It's because they know that the Pill sometimes prevents implantation that abortion advocates could honestly claim that an amendment stating human life begins at conception would effectively condemn the Pill.

The Pill's Failure to Prevent Ovulation

One of the most common misconceptions about the Pill is that its success in preventing discernible pregnancy is entirely due to its success in preventing ovulation. In fact, if a sexually active and fertile woman taking the Pill does not get pregnant in 97% of her cycles it does *not* mean she didn't ovulate in 97% of her cycles.

In many of her cycles the same woman would not have gotten pregnant even if she weren't using the Pill. Furthermore, if the Pill's second mechanism works, conception will be prevented despite ovulation taking place. If the second mechanism fails, then the third mechanism comes into play. While it may fail too, every time it succeeds it will contribute to the Pill's *perceived* contraceptive effectiveness. That is, because the child is newly conceived and tiny, and the pregnancy has just begun six days earlier, that pregnancy will not be discernible to the woman. Therefore **every time it causes an abortion the Pill will be *thought* to have succeeded as a contraceptive**. Most women will assume it has stopped them from ovulating even when it hasn't. This illusion reinforces the public's confidence in the Pill's effectiveness, with no understanding that both ovulation *and* conception may, in fact, not have been prevented at all.

In his article "Ovarian follicles during oral contraceptive cycles: their potential for ovulation," Dr. Stephen Killick says, "It is well established that newer, lower-dose regimes of combined oral contraceptive (OC) therapy do not completely suppress pituitary and ovarian function."[52]

Dr. David Sterns, in *How the Pill and the IUD Work: Gambling with Life,* states, "even the early pill formulations (which were much more likely to suppress ovulation due to their higher doses of estrogen) still allowed breakthrough ovulation to occur 1 to 3% of the time."[53] He cites an award winning study by Dutch gynecologist Dr. Nine Van der Vange in which she discovered in Pill-takers "**proof of ovulation based on ultrasound exams and hormonal indicators occurred in about 4.7% of the cycles studied.**"[54]

I obtained a copy of Dr. Van der Vange's original study, called "Ovarian activity during low dose oral contraceptives," in which she concludes,

> These findings indicate that **ovarian suppression is far from complete with the low dose OC**...Follicular development was found in a high percentage during

low-dose OC use…ovarian activity is very common for the low dose OC preparations…the mode of action of these OC is **not only based on ovulation inhibition**, but other factors are involved such as cervical mucus, vaginal pH and **composition of the endometrium**.[55]

This means that though a woman might not get clinically pregnant in 97% of her cycle months (her pregnancy able to be identified and measured through normal medical means), *there is simply no way to tell how often the Pill has actually prevented her ovulation*. Given the fact she would not get pregnant in many months even if she ovulated, and that there are at least two other mechanisms which can prevent measurable pregnancy—one contraceptive and the other abortive—a 97% apparent effectiveness rate of the Pill might mean a far lower effectiveness in actually preventing ovulation. Though we can't know exactly how much lower, it might be a 70-90% rate. The other 17-27% (these numbers are picked at random since we do not know) of the Pill's "effectiveness" could be due to a combination of the normal rates of nonpregnancy, the thickening of the cervical mucus and—at the heart of our concern here—the endometrial inhospitality to the newly conceived child.

Endometrial thickness is not the only consideration. There are a variety of hormonal factors that operate in conjunction with endometrial proliferation. Dr. Wilks explains, "The process of implantation, rather than being an accidental event dependent on chance, is in fact a multi-factorial, cascading bio-molecular, physiological and hormonal event."[56] A "hormonal dialogue" occurs between a healthy endometrium and the newly conceived child. (I refer to this elsewhere in this book.)

In an attempted refutation of my research, in an *Ethics & Medicine* Journal article titled "Redux: Is the Oral Contraceptive Pill an Abortifacient?" Dr. Joel E. Goodnough writes:

> Alcorn believes that if ovulation and conception occurs on the OCP, the embryo is at risk of being aborted due to changes in the endometrium…that are hostile to implantation of the embryo…The literature that he quotes describes the endometrium in women on the OCP as being hostile to the embryo, but no literature actually shows that death of the embryo results.[57]

But Dr. Goodnough does not cite a single research article to defend the certain or likely non-death of the embryonic child, which he apparently assumes will always somehow survive the hostile endometrium. He thus rejects the wealth of secondary and indirect evidence in favor of a position devoid of evidence. (I address Dr. Goodnough's criticisms in much more detail in *Appendix J*.)

What do the Pill Manufacturers Say?

No one is in a better position to address the question of how birth control pills work than the companies that produce them. In this section I quote from their materials and recount conversations with representatives of various Pill manufacturers.

Searle

I asked a good friend and excellent prolife physician to call a birth control pill manufacturer concerning the statements in their inserts. He contacted Searle, whose package insert for the pill Demulen, says **"alterations in the…endometrium (which may reduce the likelihood of implantation) may also contribute to the contraceptive effectiveness."** (Note that Searle twice uses the term "may," in contrast to Ortho and Wyeth, which in their information in the *PDR* state the same effect as a fact rather than a possibility.)

Here is part of a letter dated February 13, 1997, written by Barbara Struthers, Searle's Director of Healthcare Information Services, to my prolife physician friend:

> Thank you for your recent request for information regarding whether oral contraceptives are abortifacients…One of the possible mechanisms listed in the labeling is "changes in the endometrium which may reduce the likelihood of implantation." **This is a theoretical mechanism only and is not based upon experimental evidence, but upon the**

histologic appearance of the endometrium.
However, as noted by Goldzieher, the altered
endometrium is still capable of sustaining nidation, as
shown by pregnancies occurring in cycles with only a
few or no tablet omissions.[58]

Dr. Struthers (PhD) makes a valid point that the Pill's
effects on the endometrium do not *always* make
implantation impossible. But in my research I've never
found anyone who claims they *always* do. The issue
is whether they *sometimes* do. **To be an
abortifacient does not require that something
always cause an abortion, only that it sometimes
does.**

In fact, whether it's RU-486, Norplant, Depo-Provera,
the Mini-pill or the Pill, there is no chemical that
always causes an abortion. There are only those that
do so never, sometimes, often and usually. Children
who play on the freeway, climb on the roof or are left
alone by swimming pools don't *always* die, but this
hardly proves these practices are safe and never
result in fatalities. Thus, the point that the Pill doesn't
always prevent implantation is true, but has no
bearing on the question of whether it sometimes
prevents implantation, as suggested by Searle's own
literature.

Dr. Struthers goes on to say, "It is unlikely that OCs
would decrease the likelihood of endometrial
implantation, particularly when one appreciates that
the blastocyst is perfectly capable of implanting in
various 'hostile' sites, e.g. the fallopian tube, the
ovary, the peritoneum."

Her point is that the child sometimes implants in the
wrong place. True enough—but, again, no one is

41

saying this doesn't happen. The question is whether the Pill sometimes hinders the child's ability to implant in the *right* place. Whether the child implants in the wrong place or fails to implant in the right one, the result is the same—death. But in the first case a human agent does not cause the death. In the second case, it does—by use of the Pill.

Dr. Struthers then says, "Used as directed, the hormone level in modern OCs is simply too low to cause interception, that is, failure of the blastocyst to implant."

If this is true, then why does the company's own literature—produced by their researchers and submitted to the FDA, the medical community, and the public—suggest the contrary? And why do dozens and dozens of scientific and medical sources definitively state the contrary? If Dr. Struthers is right, not just some but *all* of these other sources have to be wrong.

Dr. Struthers further states; "Until the blastocyst implants…there would be no loss of an embryo and, therefore, no abortion. Thus, the theoretical mechanism of reduced likelihood of implantation by whatever means would not be considered an abortion by any biological definition."

It is here that her presuppositions become clear. Having said implantation won't be prevented, she then says even if it is, *the result isn't really an abortion*. This statement is profound both in its breadth and its inaccuracy. It's a classic logic-class-illustration of faulty reasoning. It's like saying "Sudden Infant Death Syndrome does not affect toddlers; therefore, it does not involve the deaths of human beings." Such a statement assumes facts not in evidence: that infants are not people because they are pre-toddlers. In exactly the same way Dr. Struthers assumes—without offering any evidence—that pre-embryo human beings are not really human beings.

But if human life *does* begin at conception, which is the overwhelming biological consensus, then **causing the death of a "blastocyst" is just as much an abortion as causing the death (or as she puts it, "loss") of an "embryo."** The days-old individual is a *smaller and younger* person than the embryo, but he or she is *no less* a person in the sight of God who created him. People do not get more human as they get older and bigger—if they did, toddlers would be more human than infants, adolescents more human than toddlers, adults more human than adolescents and professional basketball players more human than anyone.

Dr. Struthers says the "reduced likelihood of implantation by whatever means would not be considered an abortion by any biological definition." This statement is unscientific in the extreme. The biological definition she ignores is not just some obscure definition of life, but the precise definition, which the vast majority of scientists, including biologists, actually hold to—that life begins at conception. (See *Appendix B:* **When Does Human Life Begin? The Answer of Science.**) An early abortion is still an abortion, and no semantics change this reality, even if they manage to obscure it.

The letter from Dr. Struthers certainly contains some valid information along with the invalid. But how seriously can we take its bottom-line conclusions that the Pill is not an abortifacient? I showed her letter to one physician who told me a "healthcare information services director" is a public relations position with the primary job of minimizing controversy, denying blame, putting out fires, and avoiding any bad publicity for products, both with physicians and the general public. Perhaps this assessment was unfair—I don't know. But after reading her letter I determined to personally call the research or medical information departments of all the major birth control manufacturers and hear for myself what each of them had to say.

When I called Syntex, they informed me that Searle had recently purchased all their "feminine products," including the Pill. So I called Searle's customer service line, identified myself by name, and was asked to explain my question. When I said that it related to the Pill's mechanism of preventing implantation, the person helping me (who didn't identify herself) became discernibly uneasy. She asked me who I was, so I gave her my name again. Then she asked me to wait while she conferred with her colleagues. After several minutes she got back on the line and said "Dr. Struthers will have to talk to you about this, and she's not in."

Since Dr. Struthers was unavailable, I asked the woman if *she* could offer me any guidance. She said, uneasiness evident, "By any chance are you asking about this for religious reasons?" I said, "Yes, that's part of it." She said, "Well, I can tell you that our pills are *not* abortifacients." I asked, "Then why does your professional labeling talk about the Pill reducing the likelihood of implantation?" She said, "I can't answer that question. You'll have to talk to Dr. Struthers." I left my number, but Dr. Struthers never called me back.

Organon

Next I called Organon, the maker of the birth control pill Desogen. After explaining my question about their literature that says the Pill sometimes prevents implantation, I was transferred to Erin in medical services. She informed me "the Pill's *primary* mechanism is preventing ovulation." After my follow-up question, she said, "The other mechanisms also happen, but they're secondary." When I asked how often the primary mechanism fails and the secondary mechanisms kick in, she said "there's no way to determine the number of times which happens and which doesn't."

Reading between the lines, Erin said, "If you're asking if it's an abortifacient…[pause]" I interjected, "Yes, I am." She continued, "…that's difficult to ever say that." She added, "What happens is, if ovulation occurs, **the Pill will thicken the mucus and thin the endometrium so that it doesn't allow that pregnancy.**" She quickly added, "but it's not like the IUD." I understood her to mean that preventing implantation is the *primary* function of the IUD, whereas it is only a *secondary* function of the Pill.

Wyeth-Ayerst

Wyeth-Ayerst Labs is the maker of six combination Pills. I called and spoke with a medical information coordinator named Adrianne. I read to her the professional labeling of their Pills that says "other alterations include changes…in the endometrium (which reduce the likelihood of implantation)." I asked if she knew how often the Pill prevents implantation.

Once again it became obvious that I was prolife, presumably because no one but a prolifer would care about this issue. Adrianne read to me a printed statement that said "these mechanisms are not abortifacient in nature." She carefully explained that inhibiting ovulation and thickening the cervical mucus were contraceptive, not abortive. Of course, I agreed 100%. She then said, reading from the statement in front of her, "while it is true that progestins do alter the uterine lining, this is not considered a contraceptive action of these methods. The fact that these methods are not 100% effective and successful pregnancies have occurred clearly demonstrate that successful implantations can occur."

Over the following ten minutes, Adrianne kept talking about the first two mechanisms. I kept asking about the third. Finally she said, "Yes, that [interfering with implantation] occurs, but it doesn't prevent a pregnancy." I thought, that's true, it doesn't *prevent* a pregnancy, it actually *ends* a pregnancy, but I knew that wasn't what she meant. I then referred her back to Wyeth's professional labeling and pointed out once more the third mechanism. She followed along with her copy and said, "That third effect happens, but it's not considered a contraceptive action, because sometimes it fails to prevent pregnancy."

Of course, she had already acknowledged that sometimes the Pill fails to prevent ovulation and sometimes the thickened cervical mucus fails to prevent the sperm from fertilizing the egg. In the same way a visible pregnancy proves the third mechanism has failed, it proves the other two mechanisms have also failed. Yet *they* are still considered to be real mechanisms of the Pill, despite the fact they sometimes fail. Why shouldn't the third effect be treated the same way?

I said, "According to your professional labeling, sometimes your Pills do prevent a fertilized egg from implanting—is that correct or incorrect?" She paused for a very long time and I heard papers shuffling. Finally she said, "Yes, that's correct, but not always…that's why we can't say contraceptives are 100% effective."

I said, "Okay, let me try to summarize, and please correct me if I'm wrong. There are three different ways the Pill operates. #1 usually works. When #1 fails, #2 may work. When #1 and #2 fail, #3 may work. And sometimes all three fail."

She said "Yes, that's correct." She offered to send me information by mail, and I gladly accepted the offer. (I had asked Searle and Ortho to do this but they said they didn't have anything they could send me.) She warmly invited me to call back if I needed any more information.

When I received the information in the mail, it contained three things. The first was a cover letter written by Robin Boyle, R.Ph., Wyeth's Manager of Drug Information. It was clearly a form letter designed for those expressing concerns about abortion, and contained the precise contents that Adrianne quoted to me. Also enclosed was a colorful booklet entitled *Birth Control with the Pill*. In the section "How the Pill Works," it states, "The pill mainly prevents pregnancy in two ways." It then speaks of only the first two mechanisms and makes no reference whatsoever to the third, the prevention of implantation.

The detailed, fine print "professional labeling" was also enclosed, and, as reflected in *The PDR*, it states **"alterations include changes in...the endometrium (which reduce the likelihood of implantation)."**

It struck me that virtually everyone receiving this information would read the large print, attractive, colorful, easy-to-understand booklet (which makes no mention of the abortive mechanism), and almost no one would read the extremely small print, black and white, technically worded, and completely unattractive sheet—the one that acknowledges in the fine print that the Pill sometimes prevents implantation (thereby causing an abortion).

It is safe to say that virtually none of Wyeth's consumers will read the highly technical study printed in a 1988 *International Journal of Fertility* article, by none other than Wyeth's own Regional Director of Clinical Research, who stated one way oral contraceptives work is **"by causing endometrial changes that will not support implantation."**[59]

Ortho-McNeil

On March 24, 1997, I had a lengthy and enlightening talk with Richard Hill, a pharmacist who works for Ortho-McNeil's product information department. (Ortho-McNeil is one of the largest Pill manufacturers.) I took detailed notes.

Hill was unguarded, helpful, and straightforward. He never asked me about my religious views or my beliefs about abortion. He did not couch his language to give me an answer I wanted to hear. He couldn't, since he had no idea what biases or presuppositions I might have.

Hill informed me "I can't give you solid numbers, because there's no way to tell which of these three functions is actually preventing the pregnancy; but I can tell you the great majority of the time it's the first one [preventing ovulation]."

I asked him, "Does the Pill sometimes fail to prevent ovulation?" He said "yes." I asked, "What happens then?" He said, "The cervical mucus slows down the sperm. And if that doesn't work, **if you end up with a fertilized egg, it won't implant and grow because of the less hospitable endometrium**."

I asked him how many of the contraceptives available on the market are low-dose. He said, "I don't have statistics, but I also work in a pharmacy and I can tell you the vast majority of the time people get low-dose pills." He confirmed that there are some "higher dose" pills available, with 50 micrograms of estrogen instead of 20-35 micrograms, but said these were not commonly used. (Remember, even 50 micrograms is only 1/3 the average estrogen dosage in pills of the 1960s.)

I then asked Hill if he was *certain* the Pill made implantation less likely. "Oh, yes," he replied. I said, "So you don't think this is just a theoretical effect of the Pill?" He said the following, which I draw directly from my extensive notes of our conversation:

Oh, no, it's not theoretical. It's observable. We know what an endometrium looks like when it's rich and most receptive to the fertilized egg. When a woman is taking the Pill you can clearly see the difference,

49

based both on gross appearance—as seen with the naked eye—and under a microscope. **At the time when the endometrium would normally accept a fertilized egg, if a woman is taking the Pill it is much less likely to do so**.

I asked Hill one more time, "So you're saying this is an actual effect that happens, not just a theoretical one?" He said, "**Sure—you can actually see what it does to the endometrium and it's obvious it makes implantation less likely**. The only thing that's theoretical is the numbers, because we just don't know that."

The pills produced by Searle, Ortho, Wyeth and Organon are essentially the same thing, with only slightly different combinations of chemicals. The professional labeling is essentially the same. The medical experts at Searle, Wyeth and Organon were quick to pick up my abortion-related concerns and attempted to defuse them. Despite this, not only the pharmacist at Ortho but the medical services people at Organon and Wyeth acknowledged as an established fact what their literature says, that **the Pill sometimes prevents implantation**. Dr. Struthers of Searle appears to deny this, but then explains that if it happens it isn't really an abortion. When I stack up these responses to the wealth of information I've found in my research, I am forced to believe the people at Ortho, Wyeth, and Organon, not Dr. Struthers at Searle.

While I know that some of what she said is wrong—including the notion that preventing implantation is not a real abortion—I hope and pray that Dr. Struthers is correct and that her position is more than just a careful public relations ploy to placate known prolifers and religious people. The totality of my research, however, convinces me her position is not based on the facts.

The Pill's Third Mechanism: Real or Not?

The key point of dispute in these interviews centers on whether the Pill's prevention of implantation is theoretical or actual. None of the other three manufacturers spoke of it as anything but actual except Dr. Struthers at Searle, who said it is "a theoretical mechanism only." Pharmacist Hill at Ortho categorically stated it was "not theoretical," but based on direct, measurable observation of the endometrium. Who is correct?

Imagine a farmer who has two places where he might plant seed. One is rich, brown soil that has been tilled, fertilized and watered. The other is on hard, thin, dry and rocky soil. If the farmer wants as much seed as possible to take hold and grow, where will he plant the seed? The answer is obvious—on the fertile ground.

Now, you could say to the farmer that his preference for the rich, tilled, moist soil is based on the "theoretical," because he has probably never seen a scientific study that proves this soil is more hospitable to seed than the thin, hard, dry soil. Likely, such a study has never been done. In other words, there is no absolute proof. The farmer might reply to your skeptical challenge based on his years of observation: "I know good soil when I see it—sure, I've seen some plants grow in the hard, thin soil too, but the chances of survival are much less there than in the good soil. Call it theoretical if you want to, but anyone who knows plants and soil knows it's true!"

In fact, this "theoretical" presumption has greatly influenced reproductive medicine. Specialists who engage in *in vitro* fertilization (IVF) treat the woman hormonally in order to create a glycogen-rich, supportive endometrium. William Colliton, clinical professor of Obstetrics and Gynecology at George Washington University and Medical Center points out that "this is the type of endometrium desired by IVF practitioners to accomplish embryo transfer from the petri dish to the womb."[60]

Searle's Dr. Struthers correctly points out some newly conceived children (she would not use this term, of course) manage to survive in hostile places. But this in no way changes the obvious fact that many *more* children will survive in a richer, thicker, more hospitable endometrium than in a thinner, more inhospitable one. In this sense, the issue isn't theoretical at all.

Several articles I've read spoke of the mucus's ability to block sperm migration and presented as evidence the fact that the thickness of the mucus is visually observable. Of course, this appearance is not incontrovertible proof that it slows down sperm migration, but it is still considered valid evidence. Why would anyone accept this, yet question the evidentiary value of the endometrium's appearance?

Obviously, when the Pill thins the endometrium, and it certainly does, a zygote has a smaller likelihood of survival, a greater likelihood of death. Hence, without question a woman's taking the Pill puts any conceived child at *greater* risk of being aborted than if the Pill wasn't being taken. Other than for reasons of wishful thinking or good public relations, how can anyone seriously argue against this?

We may try to take consolation in believing that the Pill causes abortions only in theory. But we must ask, if this is a theory, how strong and credible is the theory? If the evidence is only indirect, how compelling is that indirect evidence? Once it was only a theory that plant life grows better in rich, fertile soil than in thin, eroded soil. But it was certainly a theory good farmers believed and acted on. (It is also a theory that IVF practitioners and their insurance companies—who will only pay for the most successful protocol in IVF technology—have embraced. Shouldn't that tell us something?)

Pill Manufacturer Employees Speak Up

On July 2, 1997, I interviewed Karen Witt, who worked for Whitehall-Robins, sister company of Wyeth-Ayerst, from 1986 until August 1995. Both companies are divisions of American Home Products, one of the world's largest pharmaceutical corporations.

Mrs. Witt was a sales representative who called on doctors, providing them with product samples and medical information. She worked with many popular products, including Advil and Robitussin. When the parent company acquired Wyeth-Ayerst, sales representatives were instructed to start providing physicians with samples of birth control pills. As part of their training, they were taken through a new manual that included an "Oral Contraceptive Backgrounder."

The manual, a copy of which I have in front of me, states, "The combined pill is virtually 100% effective due to a combination of the following three factors." The third of these factors is "Suppressed Endometrium," explained in this way:

> The altered hormone patterns ensure that the endometrium fails to develop to the extent found in the normal cycle. Therefore, even if "escape ovulation" should occur, **the endometrium is not in a favorable state for implantation.**[61]

When she saw this, Karen Witt realized for the first time that the Pill caused abortions. This violated her convictions. She was also concerned about something else, which she explained to me as follows:

> In company meetings information on the Pill was covered in a totally different way than other products. Our training had always been open and relaxed, and we went through detailed instruction on how every product works; we were expected to explain how they worked to physicians. But the approach to the birth control pills was completely different—the approach was, "don't worry about how they work, the point is they do; don't ask questions, just give out the samples."[62]

Karen went to her boss to express her concern, first about the Pill causing abortions, and second about the directive not to communicate important medical information to the physicians she dealt with. As a direct result of expressing these concerns, she said, "I was labeled a troublemaker." Soon, she was fired from her job of nine and a half years.

During this process, Mrs. Witt became deeply concerned as she spoke with various company employees and observed what she considered to be an agreement to remain silent about the abortive effect of their Pills.

Karen Witt pointed out to me something I'd already discovered in my dealings with Wyeth-Ayerst. The consumer pamphlet they produce, *Birth Control with the Pill,* has a section entitled "How the Pill Works" which lists only the first two mechanisms, not the third. Though both their professional labeling and their salesperson training acknowledge the third way the Pill works, in the literature given to consumers, it is simply left out.

After numerous interactions with various people at Wyeth-Ayerst, Mrs. Witt became convinced this was a deliberate cover-up on the part of the company—a cover-up not only from the general public, including users of their products, but a cover-up from physicians and pharmacists.

Mrs. Witt said to me, "I am not at all quick to use the term 'conspiracy.' But I believe there is a definite conspiracy of silence on the part of the manufacturer about the abortive effects of the Pill."

Completely unrelated to my interaction with Mrs. Witt, I was contacted by another sales representative with a major Pill manufacturer. He talked to me on the condition that I would not identify him or his company. When I asked why, he said, "They play hard ball." His story was closely parallel to Mrs. Witt's except he is still employed by the company. He believes that if he were identified he would experience retaliation from his employer.

This man read a draft of *Does the Birth Control Pill Cause Abortions?* posted at our website (www.epm.org). He called to tell me, "What you're saying about the Pill is true, and my manufacturer knows it. Management takes pride in the fact that our pills excel at the 'prevention of nidation'—that exact phrase is routinely used in our product training sessions. They never use the word 'abortion,' but by preventing nidation [implantation], that's what the pills do."

He said that in the years before the practice of using several BCPs as a "morning after" abortifacient became public, his company had instructed sales reps to inform physicians of how their pills could be used for that purpose. Because of his refusal to promote the Pill, this man was, in his words, "demoted from sales representative." Though at one point he was asked for his resignation, he says the company now seems to reluctantly accept his right to personal convictions, annoying though they may be. However, he believes he is being monitored as to what he says and to whom.

More Confirming Evidence

Intrauterine Versus Ectopic Pregnancy Ratios

Dr. Walter Larimore is an Associate Clinical Professor of Family Medicine who has written over 150 medical articles in a wide variety of journals. Dr. Larimore, in a February 26, 1998 email to me, stated that if the Pill has no negative effect on the implantation process, then we should expect its reduction in the percentage of normal intrauterine pregnancies to equal its reduction in the percentage of extrauterine or ectopic (including tubal) pregnancies.

However, Dr. Larimore pointed out something highly significant—published data from all of the studies dealing with this issue indicate that the ratio of extrauterine to intrauterine pregnancies among Pill-takers *significantly exceeds* that of non-Pill-takers. The five studies cited by Dr. Larimore show an increased risk of ectopic pregnancies in Pill takers who get pregnant, 70% to 1390% higher than non-Pill takers who get pregnant.[63][64]

What accounts for the Pill inhibiting intrauterine pregnancies at a disproportionately greater ratio than it inhibits extrauterine pregnancies? Dr. Larimore, who is a member of Focus on the Family's Physicians Resource Council, believes **the most likely explanation is that while the Pill does nothing to**

prevent a newly-conceived child from implanting in the *wrong* place (i.e. anywhere besides the endometrium) it may sometimes do something to prevent him from implanting in the *right* place (i.e. the endometrium).

This evidence puts a significant burden of proof on anyone who denies the Pill's capacity to cause early abortions. If there is an explanation of the data that is more plausible, or equally plausible, what is it?

Dr. Larimore came to this issue with significant vested interests in believing the best about the birth control pill, having prescribed it for years. When he researched it intensively over an eighteen month period, in what he described to me as a "gut wrenching" process that involved sleepless nights, he came to the conclusion that in good conscience he could no longer prescribe hormonal contraceptives, including the Pill, the minipill, Depo-Provera and Norplant.

Dr. Larimore also told me that when he has presented this evidence to audiences of secular physicians, there has been little or no resistance to it. But when he has presented it to Christian physicians there has been substantial resistance. Why? Perhaps because secular physicians do not care as much whether the Pill prevents implantation and therefore tend to be objective in interpreting the evidence. Christian physicians very much do not want to believe the Pill causes early abortions, and therefore tend to resist the evidence. This is understandable. Nonetheless, we should not permit what we *want* to believe to distract us from what the evidence indicates we *should* believe.

Three Physicians and a Pharmacist

Dr. Paul Hayes, a prolife Ob/Gyn in Lincoln, Nebraska, pointed me to Leon Speroff's and Philip Darney's authoritative text *A Clinical Guide for Contraception.* Dr. Hayes calls Dr. Speroff, of the Oregon Health Sciences University in Portland, "the nation's premier contraceptive expert and advocate." Speroff's text, written for physicians, says this:

> **The progestin in the combination pill produces an endometrium which is not receptive to ovum implantation, a decidualized bed with exhausted and atrophied glands.** The cervical mucus becomes thick and impervious to sperm transport. It is possible that progestational influences on secretion and peristalsis within the fallopian tube provide additional contraceptive effects.[65]

In an email to me dated February 22, 1997, Dr. Hayes pointed out a semantic aspect of Dr. Speroff's statement, which I, not being a physician, wouldn't have noticed:

> I was struck dumb when I read this, at the fact that Dr. Speroff would expect me, as a doctor, to accept the 'implantation' of an 'ovum.' Call it a *fertilized* ovum, or a blastocyst, or a zygote, or any one of a number of other dehumanizing names for a baby, but don't warrant to me, in a textbook for doctors, that what implants is just an ovum![66]

Dr. Hayes's point is that "ovum" used without a qualifier always means an unfertilized egg, and that Dr. Speroff is misusing the term consciously or unconsciously to minimize the taking of human life inherently involved in the preventing of implantation.

This type of semantic alteration is common in later stages, as demonstrated by references to "terminating a pregnancy" instead of "killing a child." It is further illustrated in the fact that Dr. Speroff includes as a form of "contraception" the destruction of an already conceived person.

In an interview conducted by Denny Hartford, director of Vital Signs Ministries, Pharmacist Larry Frieders, who is also vice president of Pharmacists for Life, said this:

> Obviously, the one "back-up mechanism" [of the Pill] that we're most concerned with is the one that changes the woman's body in such a way that if there is a new life, that tiny human loses the ability to implant and then grow and be nourished by the mother. The facts are clear—we've all known them intellectually. I learned them in school. I had to answer those questions on my state board pharmacy exam. The problem was getting that knowledge from my intellect down to where it became part of who I am. I had to accept that I was participating in the sale and distribution of a product that was, in fact, causing the loss of life.[67]

Later in the same interview, Hartford asked world famous fertility specialist Dr. Thomas Hilgers, "Are there any birth control pills out there that do not have this potential to abort a developing child?" Dr. Hilgers answered,

> There are none! At my last count in looking at the *Physicians Desk Reference*…there were 44 different types of birth control pills…and they have different concentrations of chemicals that make them work. None of these so-called birth control pills has a mechanism which is completely contraceptive. Put the

other way around, **all birth control pills available have a mechanism which disturbs or disintegrates the lining of the uterus to the extent that the possibility of abortion exists when breakthrough ovulation occurs.**[68]

Not One, but Five Elements of Risk

Sources indicate not only that Pill-induced endometrial changes prevent implantation (what I will call the Pill's first abortive effect), but, and this is a second abortive effect, that even if they do allow implantation they can prevent the proper nourishment or maintenance of the new child, resulting in a premature end of the pregnancy.[69]

In *My Body, My Health*, the authors point to a third abortive potential of the Pill:

Estrogen and progestin may also alter the pattern of muscle contractions in the tubes and uterus. **This may interfere with implantation by speeding up the fertilized egg's travel time so that it reaches the uterus before it is mature enough to implant.**[70]

This is the same "contraceptive" effect Dr. Speroff referred to as "peristalsis within the fallopian tube."

In its 1984 publication "Facts About Oral Contraceptives," the U.S. Department of Health and Human Services stated,

Both kinds of pills…make it difficult for a fertilized egg to implant, by causing changes in fallopian tube contractions and in the uterine lining.[71]

These changes in fallopian tube contractions can cause a failure to implant. This third abortive effect is distinct from the first two, both of which are caused by changes to the uterine lining. (Those who remain unconvinced about the abortive effect of Pill-caused endometrial changes must also address the separate but significant issue of tubal peristalsis.)

There's a fourth potential abortive threat, pointed out to me by a couple that stopped using their pills after reading the package insert. I have that insert in front of me. It concerns Desogen, a combination pill produced by Organon. Under the heading "Pregnancy Due to Pill Failure," it states:

> The incidence of pill failure resulting in pregnancy is approximately one percent (i.e., one pregnancy per 100 women per year) if taken every day as directed, but more typical failure rates are about 3%. If failure does occur, the **risk to the fetus is minimal**.[72]

Exactly what *is* this risk to the fetus? I asked this of Dr. William Toffler of the Oregon Health Sciences University, who is also a member of Focus on the Family's Physician's Resource Council. Dr. Toffler informed me that the hormones in the Pill, progestin and estrogen, can sometimes have a harmful effect on an already implanted child. The problem is, since women do not know they are pregnant in the earliest stages, they will continue to take the Pill at least one more time, if not two or more (especially if cycles are irregular). This creates the risk the leaflet refers to. So not only is the pre-implanted child at risk, but so is an *already implanted child* who is subjected to the Pill's hormones.

The risk is called "minimal." But what does this mean? If someone was about to give your child a chemical and they assured you there was a "minimal risk," would you allow them to proceed without investigating to find out exactly what was meant by "minimal"? Wouldn't you ask whether there was some alternative treatment without this risk? Rather than be reassured by the term "minimal," a parent might respond, "I didn't know that by taking the Pill I caused *any* risk to a baby—so when you tell me the risk is 'minimal' you don't reassure me, you alarm me."

There is still a fifth risk, which is distinct in that it applies to children conceived *after* a woman stops taking the Pill:

> There is some indication that **there may be a prolonged effect of the oral contraceptives on both the endometrium and the cervix after a woman has ceased taking the pill**. There may well be a greater likelihood of miscarriage in that period also as a result of some chromosomal abnormalities…It is worth noting that the consumer advice from the manufacturers cautions that pregnancy should be avoided in the first three months after ceasing the combined oral contraceptive.[73]

Why should pregnancy be avoided until three months after a woman has stopped using the Pill? One physician told me it's because the Pill produces an environment that threatens the welfare of a child, *and* **that environment takes months to return to normal**. If those effects are still considered a risk up to three months after the Pill was last taken, it also confirms the risks to both the pre- and post-implantation child while the Pill is still being used. Another physician suggested that abnormal eggs are more likely after Pill use and that is one reason for the warning.

(This should serve as a warning to couples that choose to stop taking the pill out of concern for its abortifacient potential. If they remain sexually active, they should use a non-abortive contraceptive for three months to allow time for the endometrium to return to normal. Otherwise, since the abortive mechanism may remain operative after the contraceptive mechanisms no longer are, for that brief period they could actually increase their chances of an abortion.)

The Morning-After Pill:
Standard BCPs

In June 1996 the Food and Drug Administration announced a new use for standard combination birth control pills:

> Two high doses taken within two to three days of intercourse can prevent pregnancy, the FDA scientists said. Doctors think the pills probably work by **preventing a fertilized egg from implanting in the lining of the uterus**.[74]

On February 24, 1997, the FDA approved the use of high doses of combination birth control pills as "emergency contraception."[75] The article explains,

> The morning-after pill refers to a regimen of standard birth control pills taken within 72 hours of unprotected sex to prevent an unwanted pregnancy. The pills prevent pregnancy **by inhibiting a fertilized egg from implanting itself in the uterus** and developing into a fetus.[76]

Of course, the pills do *not* "prevent pregnancy" since pregnancy begins at conception, not implantation. Acting as if pregnancy begins at implantation takes the emphasis off the baby's objective existence and puts it on the mother's endometrium and its role in sustaining the child that has already been created within her. As *World* magazine points out, "In reality the pill regimen—designed to block a fertilized egg from implanting into the uterus—aborts a pregnancy that's already begun."[77]

It is significant that this "morning after pill" is in fact nothing but a combination of several standard birth control pills taken in high dosages. When the announcement was made, the uninformed public probably assumed that the high dosage makes birth control pills do something they were otherwise incapable of doing. But the truth is that **it simply increases the chances of doing what it already sometimes does—cause an abortion**.

A 1999 press release from the American College of Obstetricians and Gynecologists (ACOG) asserts the following:

> Many pharmacies…refuse to provide the [emergency contraception] based on the incorrect belief that it is an abortifacient…. [The] **EC works by preventing ovulation, fertilization or the implantation of the fertilized egg into the uterus.**[78]

Later in the same press release the ACOG argues, "this [refusal to sell EC] makes absolutely no sense" because one large national pharmacy chain that refuses to carry it "already dispenses emergency contraception in the form of other prescription oral contraceptives."

In a *USA Today* article, "Docs spread word: Pill works on morning after," Marilyn Elias wrote,

> U.S. gynecologists are launching a major nationwide campaign to make sure women know about the best-kept morning-after contraceptive secret: common birth control pills…Some oral contraceptives may be taken after intercourse—two in the first dose up to 72 hours after sex, then two more 12 hours later—and will prevent 75% of pregnancies…Critics call the morning-after method de facto abortion, but Zinberg says the

pills work before an embryo implants in the uterus so there's no abortion.[79]

This is another illustration of the role of semantics in minimizing our perception of the true nature of chemical abortions. The truth is, these pregnancies aren't prevented; they are *terminated*. It's semantic gymnastics to redefine abortion in such a way that killing the "fertilized egg" doesn't qualify.

Life does not begin at implantation; it begins at conception. To suggest that a fertilized egg is not a living person just because she has not yet settled into her home (the endometrium), and therefore it's fine to make her home hostile to her life, is like saying the homeless are not really people since they aren't living in a house, and it's therefore all right to burn down homes they might otherwise have lived in, and to leave them out in the cold to die.

Consider the following in a medical journal article that responds to the question, "Must a Catholic hospital inform a rape victim of the availability of the 'morning-after pill'?"

> Diethylstilbestrol, and other estrogens used after unprotected coitus, acts to prevent implantation of a fertilized ovum in the uterine mucosa…Thus these drugs are neither contraceptives nor abortifacients. From a medical viewpoint, pregnancy begins at the completion of implantation, and the accurate way to describe the action of the morning-after pill is "pregnancy interception."[80]

"Pregnancy interception" is still another term that obscures what really happens in a chemical abortion. Define pregnancy however you wish, but it does not change the fact there is a living child prior to implantation.

Webster's 1984 ninth edition *New Collegiate Dictionary* defines the word conception as "the act of becoming pregnant." Yet many sources I have consulted, including the above, admit the Pill can allow conception and prevent implantation, but insist on describing this as "preventing pregnancy."
The truth is, whatever prevents implantation kills the same unique human being as any later abortion procedure. The terms this is couched in may make it sound better, but they cannot change what it really is.

Evidence to the Contrary?

Is there any evidence refuting the abortive potential of the Pill? I have searched far and wide to find such evidence myself, and have also asked a number of physicians to provide me with any they have or know of. What I have managed to find, I will now present.

In several cases, I deliberately do not state the names of Christian physicians and organizations that have written some of the letters and articles I am citing. I know this is unusual, but I am determined not to create unnecessary hostility or disunity. I have no desire to put any brother or sister in Christ on the spot, nor do I want to run the risk of making them more defensive of their position. In cases where I have not mentioned names, I must ask the reader to trust that I have the actual documents in front of me.

An interview with Physicians

"Advances in Oral Contraception" in *The Journal of Reproductive Medicine*, is a question and answer session with eight physicians. The prolife physician who gave this to her pastor underlined statements that in her mind refute the notion that the Pill causes abortions. This is one of them:

> Do the OCs with 30 micrograms of estrogen act primarily by preventing implantation rather than suppressing ovulation?
>
> Dr. Christie: "Our studies in Europe and Canada showed that the 150/30 pill's main mode of action is inhibition of ovulation."[81]

This statement is not in conflict with the evidence I've presented. No one disputes whether the inhibition of ovulation is the Pill's *main* mode of action, only whether preventing implantation is a secondary mode. A more significant segment of the same article is this:

Are factors besides anovulation [not ovulating] affected by the contraceptive action of the Pill?

Dr. Christie: Yes—cervical mucus, maybe nidation, the endometrium, so it's not in the appropriate condition for receiving a fertilized ovum. The authorities agree that with the LH and FSH changes, no ovulation occurs; the egg isn't there to be fertilized.

Dr. Goldzieher: Some time ago Pincus found, when studying Enovid 5 and 10, that conceptions occurred with these pills. To me his evidence indicates that there must not be much of an antiimplantation effect on the endometrium if a woman can skip a very-high-dose OC for a few days and become pregnant. If there is an antiimplantation effect, it certainly is absent in some cases.[82]

These statements are significant, but they only *qualify* the mountain of other evidence, they do not *refute* it. Dr. Christie acknowledges the antiimplantation effect of the Pill, but says that with the proper chemical changes no ovulation occurs. He is surely not claiming that these chemical changes *always* happen in the intended way, nor is he denying that ovulations occur among Pill-takers. He is well aware that pregnancies occur, as Dr. Goldzieher confirms in the very next sentence. Obviously, for every measurable pregnancy there are a number of breakthrough ovulations.

Dr. Goldzieher, whose own work, cited elsewhere in this book, acknowledges the antiimplantation effect, affirms that, "it certainly is absent in some cases." Ironically, this quotation assumes the very thing the physician giving the letter to her pastor was trying to assure him wasn't true. When you say the effect of preventing implantation is absent in some cases, you are implying it is present in some cases. (In any case, a physician wrote to me that the high-dose Enovid Goldzieher refers to is no longer made.)

Again, no one claims the Pill's diminishing of the endometrium *always* makes implantation impossible. Obviously it doesn't. The issue is whether it *sometimes* does. That plants can and do grow through cracks in driveways does not negate the fact that they will more likely grow in the tilled, fertile soil of the garden. The Pill's changing the endometrium from fertile to inhospitable does not always result in an abortion, but sometimes it does. And "sometimes" is all it takes.

Letters from Prolife Physicians

I have before me a four-page letter from a prolife physician, assuring the recipient that the Pill, Norplant and Depo-Provera are not abortifacients, while RU-486, the "morning after pill" and the "minipill" are abortifacient. The letter is well crafted, but it is missing a crucial element—it does not cite a single study or produce any evidence whatsoever to back up any of its claims!

In the absence of any such evidence, I am forced to conclude that this letter is simply a sincere expression of the physician's personal beliefs. Unfortunately, beliefs do not constitute evidence.

When I submitted to him a half dozen of the sources I've cited in this book, a prolife physician wrote this to me:

> It is known fact that 6% of women on BCPs will become pregnant while on the pill, meaning that cervical mucous failed, ovulation occurred, and implantation was successful. This implies that when BCPs don't work, it is because they totally fail, and that when mechanisms 1 and 2 don't work, implantation is not prevented by the BCPs causing an early abortion. If I believed BCPs worked by causing abortion, I wouldn't recommend them. I firmly believe that when they work, they work by preventing ovulation and by creation of thick cervical mucus.

I do not question this physician's sincerity, but I do question his logic. We do not know how often mechanism number one, two or three actually work. We only know that sometimes all three fail. But because number one and two *sometimes* fail, no one therefore concludes that they *always* fail. So why conclude that because number three sometimes fails, therefore it always fails?

How can we look at a known pregnancy, which proves the failure of all three mechanisms, then conclude that number one and number two *normally* work, but number three *never* works? The logic escapes me. If number three didn't involve an abortion, I don't think anyone would deny it happens. It appears this denial is not prompted by any real evidence, but by the desire the evidence not be true.

Letters from Christian Organizations

A number of people have sent me responses from Christian organizations they have received after writing to ask if the Pill really causes abortions. These letters raise various arguments, which I address in the "Objections" section at the end of this book.

One of these letters states that the Pill "rarely, if ever, permits conception."

The term "if ever" is certainly false, since the BCP manufacturers themselves admit 3% of those taking the Pill experience a pregnancy in any given year. In fact, recent research indicates that figure may be considerably higher—up to 4% for "good compliers" and 8% for "poor compliers."[83]

The letter goes on to say, "criticism of oral contraception heaps needless guilt upon women who literally cannot use any other method of contraception—guilt which seems especially unnecessary…"

The letter does not deal with the issue of what is true nearly as much as the issue of how bad some people feel when they hear that the Pill causes abortions. The letter, from a fine organization, goes on to say this:

> Our programming staff has come to the conclusion that it might be wisest to avoid further discussions of this subject on the air. The last time we offered such a broadcast, the ensuing mail revealed how very wide is the array of opinions that exists among committed

believers is this area . . . It seems we are bound to offend someone as soon as we open our mouths, and we continue to receive criticism from listeners with differing perspectives despite our attempts to present a balanced treatment of the subject. This is why we have no plans for future programs of this kind.

I believe the writer honestly thought he answered the inquiry. In fact, he did little more than point out the variety of opinions within the Christian community, without offering evidence to suggest which might be right. While the letter gave the clear impression that the Pill does not cause abortions, it did not cite any evidence to indicate it does not, and did nothing to refute the substantial evidence that it does.

Another letter, written by a different person at the same organization, was emphatic:

We have consulted with medical advisors who have reviewed a wealth of competent, scientific research on this issue. In their opinion, these studies suggest that the Pill does not act as an abortifacient; rather it works solely by preventing ovulation. Even in the rare event that conception takes place, they do not believe that it is accurate to attribute the possibility of the conceptus failing to implant to the action of the Pill.

Some recipients of such a letter will come away assured they now know the truth about the Pill—it never causes abortions. Unfortunately, while sounding credible, the letter makes a provably false statement (that the Pill "works solely by preventing ovulation"). Furthermore, it does not offer a single reference to so much as a quote, name, book, article, lecture or any source whatsoever to back up its claims.

We called the organization to inquire concerning the identity of *any* of this "wealth of competent, scientific research" that supports this definitive statement that the Pill doesn't cause abortions. I was very eager to examine such material. Both writers of these letters are no longer with this organization, and the person we spoke with was not aware of any such research and could not point us toward it. (Certainly, if such information exists, the research departments of the Pill manufacturers are not aware of it. If they were, they would cite it when called by people like myself whose minds would be relieved by any evidence that the Pill doesn't cause abortions.)

Though I am not questioning integrity or motives, it is particularly unfortunate when a Christian organization gives incomplete, inaccurate and misleading information to those inquiring about the Pill because they sincerely want to avoid jeopardizing the lives of unborn children.

Article in a Christian Magazine

Writing in a popular women's magazine, a Christian family physician states that some people have expressed concern that non-barrier birth control methods may prevent implantation. He then says this:

> While not at all like the deliberate destruction of the growing fetus that occurs during a "therapeutic" abortion, this interruption of the earliest stages of human life could be considered an unintentional abortion.[84]

"*Could* be considered an unintentional abortion"? How could it be considered anything else? "*Not at all* like the deliberate destruction of the growing fetus"? It

75

may not be deliberate, but that doesn't make it utterly unlike later abortions. It is unlike them in *intent*, but exactly like them in *effect*—both kill a child. (The child who dies is also "growing," just like the "fetus" in later abortions.)

The same physician says this concerning the Pill:

> The possibility of an "unfriendly uterus" preventing pregnancy has long been mentioned in the standard FDA-approved product literature for oral contraceptives, but a number of researchers aren't convinced this takes place. Overall, the likelihood of such unintentional abortions appears to be extremely remote, if not infinitesimal.[85]

The author does not cite studies from any of these unconvinced researchers, nor does he identify them. The only evidence he presents for abortions being "extremely remote" is that "the fertilized egg actually appears to be quite proficient at burrowing into the lining of the uterus." He says that this is demonstrated by women who become pregnant after missing a single dose of the Pill and even after not missing any at all.

Once again, the fact that implantation sometimes takes place despite the Pill's creation of an inhospitable endometrium in no way negates the fact that it occurs more often in a hospitable endometrium.

Speech by a Prolife Physician

A reader sent me a photocopied page from an article, but unfortunately the name and date of the publication isn't included and I have been unable to trace it. The article is an excerpt from a speech by a prolife physician named Dr. Mastroianni:

> "It's also important," Dr. Mastroianni added, "when talking about oral contraception, to dispel any idea that the pill acts as an abortifacient. Propaganda has led some people to believe that somehow the pill works after fertilization, and that's further from the truth than anything I can think of. The pill works by inhibiting ovulation, as well as by thickening the cervical mucus and therefore inhibiting sperm migration."[86]

This confident claim is made without the offer of any evidence to support it. Leveling the accusation of "propaganda" is not the same as presenting evidence, or refuting it.

When the scientific and medical sources, including not just reference books but studies reported in medical journals over decades, consistently affirm there is an anti-implantation effect of the Pill, how can a physician state this to be "further from the truth than anything I can think of"? When these sources consistently and repeatedly conclude there are at least three ways the Pill works—one of which is clearly abortive—how can someone definitively say there are *really* only two?

I do not consider this quotation from a well-meaning prolife physician as evidence of anything but the human tendency to deny something we do not wish to believe. (If a reader knows Dr. Mastroianni, and he *does* have evidence for his beliefs, I would very much like to see it, and will gladly revise this book accordingly.)

Clinical Experience

Dr. William Colliton, who is convinced of the abortifacient nature of the Pill, refers to some anecdotal experience that may contribute toward the general belief of many physicians that no abortions occur while a woman is on the Pill. With regard to clinical evidence he writes that the physician may "note that the typical clinical picture of spontaneous abortion (heavy bleeding, severe cramping, passage of tissue) is rarely, if ever, seen by practicing physicians caring for patients on the Pill."

He then writes,

> They seem to overlook the fact that the abortions caused by the BCP occur when the baby is 5 to 14-16 days old and that the lining of the uterus is 'less vascular, less glandular, thinner' than normal as they describe it. From the clinical perspective, one would anticipate a non-event.[87]

In other words, the fact that a treating physician does not see typical symptoms related to miscarriage is no proof that an abortion has not occurred. After all, a side effect of the Pill is amenorrhea; the uterine environment is changed so that there is "no menstrual flow when on the break from the hormones."[88] These changes exclude normal symptoms of miscarriage, and therefore the lack of those symptoms proves nothing.

Study on Norplant's Damage to Ova

One physician presented me with a study of Norplant, which he believes calls into question the concept of an inhospitable endometrium:

> As with other hormonal contraceptives, Norplant use is associated with suppressed endometrial development…Ovulation inhibition is the primary mechanism of Norplant's contraceptive action. Ovulation may occur, however, in about 45% of the cycles of long-term users of Norplant…at least two alternative mechanisms can be postulated…the hostility of the cervical mucus to sperm penetration, and impaired maturation of the oocyte, rendering it nonfertilizable because of low levels of follicle-stimulating hormone and LH that occur during use of Norplant.[89]

The authors believe that given their method of study "it would have been possible to identify menstrual abortions if they had occurred." They state such evidence was absent. The article ends by saying; "We conclude from these data that postfertilization interruption of early pregnancy (menstrual abortion) does not play a role in the mechanism of action of Norplant."

Because both contain progestin, the physician who showed me the study felt the conclusion pertained not only to Norplant, but the Pill. There are several problems here. First, the study was done on Norplant, *not* the Pill. While both have progestin, they are not the same product—Norplant's operative chemical is progestin only, while the combination pill also contains estrogen. The chemical amounts, how they assimilate into the body and other factors differ between the two products. This study's results do not correspond to those of many other studies of Norplant, and it may or may not be authenticated by further studies. In any case, studies on Norplant and the Pill are not interchangeable.

Second, the fact remains that some women taking Norplant get pregnant. Obviously, then, ova are not always damaged, and are not always incapable of being fertilized. Hence, the "damaged egg" mechanism, like all others, does not always work.

Third, this study was done on only thirty-two women. This is too small a sampling to reach definitive conclusions. Studies with small test groups may be helpful as confirmations of established research, but they are not sufficient to warrant significant changes in conclusions, apart from larger studies showing them to be valid.

Fourth, if it has any pertinence at all to the Pill, which is uncertain, this study would have to be weighed against all the other sources, not to mention common sense, that connect an atrophied endometrium to a smaller likelihood of implantation. All the Pill manufacturers, who have done by far the most research on the matter, conclude that the Pill produces an inhospitable endometrium that reduces the likelihood of implantation. It would take considerably more evidence than this small study— and evidence directly pertaining to the Pill, not Norplant—to stack up against the established evidence that the Pill causes abortions.

Statement by 20 Prolife OB-GYN Specialists who are pro-Pill

A strong statement against the idea that the Pill can cause abortions was issued in January 1998, five months after the original printing of this book. (And, it has been suggested to me, largely in response to it.) According to a January 30, 1998 email sent me by one of its circulators, the statement "is a collaborative effort by several very active pro-life OB-GYN specialists, and screened through about twenty additional OB-GYN specialists."

The statement is entitled "Birth Control Pills: Contraceptive or Abortifacient?" Those wishing to read it in its entirety, which I recommend, can find it at our EPM web page, at www.epm.org/doctors.html. I have posted it there because while I disagree with its major premise and various statements in it, I believe it deserves a hearing.

The title is somewhat misleading, in that it implies there are only two ways to look at the Pill: always a contraceptive or always an abortifacient. In fact, I know of no one who believes it is always an abortifacient. There are only those who believe it is always a contraceptive and never an abortifacient, and those who believe it is usually a contraceptive and *sometimes* an abortifacient. (This misleading title sets up a straw man argument, since it is easy to prove the Pill does not always cause abortions.)

The paper opens with this statement:

> Currently the claim that hormonal contraceptives [birth control pills, implants (Norplant), injectables

(DepoProvera)] include an abortifacient mechanism of action is being widely disseminated in the pro-life community. This theory is emerging with the assumed status of "scientific fact," and is causing significant confusion among both lay and medical pro-life people. With this confusion in the ranks comes a significant weakening of both our credibility with the general public and our effectiveness against the tide of elective abortion.[90]

The question of whether the presentation of research and medical opinions, such as those in this book, causes "confusion" is interesting. Does it cause confusion, or does it bring to light pertinent information in an already existing state of confusion? Would we be better off to uncritically embrace what we have always believed than to face evidence that may challenge it?

Is our credibility and effectiveness weakened through presenting evidence that indicates the Pill can cause abortions? I'll come back to this and related objections later, but I think we need to commit ourselves to discovering and sharing the truth regardless of whether it is well-received by the general public or the Christian community.

The physicians' statement's major thesis is this—the idea that the Pill causes a hostile endometrium is a myth:

Over time, the descriptive term "hostile endometrium" progressed to be an unchallenged assumption, then to be quasi-scientific fact, and now, for some in the pro-life community, to be a proof text. And all with no demonstrated scientific validation.[91]

When I showed this to one professor of family medicine he replied, "This is an amazing claim." Why? Because, he pointed out, it requires that every physician who has directly observed the dramatic pill-induced changes in the endometrium, and every textbook that refers to these changes, has been wrong all along in believing what appears to be obvious: that when the zygote attaches itself to the endometrium its chances of survival are greater if what it attaches to is thick and rich in nutrients and oxygen than if it is not.

This is akin to announcing to a group of farmers that all these years they have been wrong to believe the myth that rich fertilized soil is more likely to foster and maintain plant life than thin eroded soil.

It could be argued that if anything may cause prolifers to lose credibility, at least with those familiar with what the Pill does to the endometrium, it is to claim the Pill does nothing to make implantation less likely.

The authors defend their position this way:

> [The blastocyst] has an invasive nature, with the demonstrated ability to invade, find a blood supply, and successfully implant on various kinds of tissue, whether "hostile," or even entirely "foreign" to its usual environment—decidualized (thinned) endometrium, tubal epithelium (lining), ovarian epithelium (covering), cervical epithelium (lining), even peritoneum (abdominal lining cells)…The presumption that implantation of a blastocyst is thwarted by "hostile endometrium" is contradicted by the "pill pregnancies" we as physicians see.[92]

This is very similar to the argument of Dr. Struthers at Searle, the Pill-manufacturer. Unfortunately, it misses the point, since the question is not whether the zygote sometimes implants in the wrong place. Of course it does. The question, rather, is whether the newly-conceived child's chances of survival are greater when it implants in the right place (endometrium) that is thick and rich and full of nutrients than in one which lacks these qualities because of the Pill. To point out a blastocyst is capable of implanting in a fallopian tube or a thinned endometrium is akin to pointing to a seed that begins to grow on asphalt or springs up on the hard dry path. Yes, the seed is thereby shown to have an invasive nature. But surely no one believes its chances of survival are as great on a thin hard rocky path as in cultivated fertilized soil.

According to the statement signed by the twenty physicians, "The entire 'abortifacient' presumption, therefore, depends on 'hostile endometrium'." Actually this isn't true, since one of the apparent abortifacient effects of the Pill is what Dr. Leon Speroff and others refer to as peristalsis within the fallopian tube. This effect speeds up the blastocyst's travel so it can reach the uterus before it's mature enough to implant. Even if the endometrium was not altered to become inhospitable, this effect could still cause abortions. (It would be accurate to say that the abortifacient belief is based *mainly*, though not entirely, on the concept of an inhospitable endometrium.)

In fact, one need not embrace the term "hostile" endometrium to believe the Pill can cause abortions. It does not take a hostile or even an inhospitable endometrium to account for an increase in abortions. It only takes a *less* hospitable endometrium. Even if they feel "hostile" is an overstatement, can anyone

84

seriously argue that the Pill-transformed endometrium is not *less* hospitable to implantation than the endometrium at its rich thick nutrient-laden peak in a normal cycle uninfluenced by the Pill?

A professor of family medicine told me that until reading this statement he had never heard, in his decades in the field, *anyone* deny the radical changes in the endometrium caused by the Pill and the obvious implications this has for reducing the likelihood of implantation. This is widely accepted as obvious and self-evident. According to this physician, the fact that secular sources embrace this reality and only prolife Christians are now rejecting it (in light of the recent attention on the Pill's connection to abortions) suggests they may be swayed by vested interests in the legitimacy of the Pill.

The paper states "there are no scientific studies that we are aware of which substantiate this presumption [that the diminished endometrium is less conducive to implantation]." But it doesn't cite any studies, or other evidence, that suggest otherwise.

In fact, surprisingly, though the statement that was sent to me is five pages long it contains not a single reference to any source that backs up any of its claims. If observation and common sense have led people in medicine to a particular conclusion over decades, should their conclusion be rejected out of hand without citing specific research indicating it to be incorrect?

On which side does the burden of proof fall—the one that claims the radically diminished endometrium inhibits implantation or the one that claims it doesn't?

The most potentially significant point made in the paper is this:

> The ectopic rate in the USA is about 1% of all pregnancies. Since an ectopic pregnancy involves a preimplantation blastocyst, both the "on pill conception" and normal "non pill conception" ectopic rate should be the same—about I% (unaffected by whether the endometrium is "hostile" or "friendly.") Ectopic pregnancies in women on hormonal contraception (except for the minipill) are practically unreported. **This would suggest conception on these agents is quite rare.** If there are millions of "on-pill conceptions" yearly, producing millions of abortions, (as some "BC pill is abortifacient" groups allege), **we would expect to see a huge increase in ectopics in women on hormonal birth control. We don't.** Rather, as noted above, this is a rare occurrence.[93]

The premise of this statement is right on target. It is exactly the premise proposed by Dr. Walter Larimore, which I've already presented. While the statement's premise is correct, its account of the data, unfortunately, is not. The five studies pointed to by Dr. Larimore, cited earlier, clearly demonstrate the statement is incorrect when it claims ectopic pregnancies in women on hormonal contraception are "practically unreported" and "rare."

This book makes no claims as to the total numbers of abortions caused by the Pill. But the statement signed by the twenty physicians affirms that *if* the Pill caused millions of abortions we would "expect to see a huge increase in ectopics in women on hormonal birth control." **In fact, that is exactly what we *do* see**—an increase that five major studies put between 70% and 1390%.

Ironically, when we remove the statement's incorrect data about the ectopic pregnancy rate and plug in the correct data, **the statement supports the very thing it attempts to refute**. It suggests the Pill may indeed cause early abortions, possibly a very large number of them.

I have been told that the above statement from prolife physicians was sent to every prolife pregnancy center in the country in an attempt to reassure them that the talk about the Pill sometimes causing abortions is inaccurate and misguided. Unfortunately, the statement itself was poorly researched and misleading. However, pregnancy centers receiving the statements did not know this. Many were understandably impressed with the list of prolife physicians apparently agreeing with the statement. Unfortunately, it appears that very few of these physicians actually researched the issue. They appear to have relied almost completely on the sincerely believed but faulty research of a few.

Statement by 26 Prolife OB-GYN Specialists who believe the Pill causes abortions

In response to the strong statement put forth by twenty of their well-respected colleagues, another collaborative statement was issued at the 1998 mid-winter gathering of the American Association of Prolife Obstetricians and Gynecologists (AAPLOG). Opening the debate, Dr. Pamela Smith stated,

> ...it has become glaringly apparent that now is the time for us, as an organization, to sail into the dangerous and uncharted waters that we have

perhaps intentionally avoided. These are the "waters" of prolife principles as they relate to fertility control.

I have intentionally used the words "fertility control" rather than contraception for a number of reasons. Foremost of which is the raging moral, biological and scientific debate, almost exclusively within the prolife community, as to whether the mechanism of certain fertility control measures are contraceptive or abortifacient at a microscopic level.[94]

The AAPLOG convention concluded with a document that includes the following statement:

> The undersigned [26 OB-GYN specialists] believe that the **facts as detailed in this document indicate the abortifacient nature of hormonal contraception**. This is supported by the scientific work of the Alan Guttmacher Institute which can, in no way, be confused with a right-to-life organization. We also want to make it clear that we have no desire to cause confusion and division among prolife forces. However, we do want to make it clear that we do desire that all women using the Pill are truthfully and fully informed about all its modes of action [including abortifacient].[95]

A complete article entitled "Birth Control Pill: Abortifacient and Contraceptive" by William F. Colliton, Jr., M.D., FACOG, which includes the above statements can be found at the EPM web page www.epm.org/26doctor.html.

It should go without saying that the latter statement should not be regarded as more credible simply because it has been signed on to by six more OB-GYNs than the prior one. The point is not numbers (26 people can be wrong as easily as 20) but accuracy of research and evidence. I believe that on close inspection (unfortunately this rarely takes place) nearly all objective parties would agree that the second statement is based on sounder science than the first.

I do not know how many pregnancy centers have received or read this second document. I do know, as of late in 2000, many sincere prolifers are still citing the earlier statement and continue to make inaccurate statements such as "There's really no evidence the Pill can cause abortions" or even "it's been proven by doctors that the Pill is never an abortifacient." I wish these statements were true. Unfortunately, they are not.

How often Does the Pill Cause Abortions?

Why It's So Difficult to Know for Sure

How many abortions does the Pill cause? This is difficult to determine. The answer depends on how often the Pill fails to prevent ovulation, and how often when ovulation fails and pregnancy occurs, the third mechanism prevents a fertilized egg from implanting.

I posed the question to Dr. Harry Kraus, a physician and writer of popular novels with medical themes. This was his response in a December 23, 1996 email:

> How often do birth control pills prevent pregnancy by causing the lining of the uterus to be inhospitable to implantation? You will not see an answer to that question anywhere, with our present state of the science. The reason is that we can only detect early pregnancy by a hormone, beta-hcg (Human chorionic gonadotropin), which is produced by the embryo after implantation. After fertilization, implantation does not take place for approximately six days. After implantation, it takes another six days before the embryo (trophoblast) has invaded the maternal venous system so that a hormone (beta-hcg) made by the embryo can reach and be measured in the mom's blood. Therefore, the statistic you seek is not available.[96]

Determining Breakthrough Ovulation Rates

Despite the fact that definitive numbers cannot be determined, there are certain medical evidences that provide rationale for estimating the numbers of Pill-induced abortions. Determining the rate of breakthrough ovulation in Pill-takers is one key to coming up with informed estimates.

In his *Abortifacient Contraception: The Pharmaceutical Holocaust*, Dr. Rudolph Ehmann says,

> As early as 1967, at a medical conference, the representatives of a major hormone producer admitted that with OCs [oral contraceptives], ovulation with a possibility of fertilization took place in up to seven percent of cases, and that subsequent implantation of the fertilized egg would usually be prevented.[97]

Bogomir M. Kuhar, Doctor of Pharmacy, is the president of Pharmacists for Life. He cites studies suggesting oral contraceptives have a breakthrough ovulation rate of 2 to 10%.[98]

World-renowned fertility specialist Dr. Thomas Hilgers estimates the breakthrough ovulation rate at 4 to 10%.[99]

Dr. Nine van der Vange, at the Society for the Advancement of Contraception's November 26-30, 1984 conference in Jakarta, stated that her studies indicated an ovulation rate of 4.7% for women taking the Pill.[100]

In another study, 14% of Pill-taking women experienced escape ovulation.[101] However, this involved only twenty-two women, with three experiencing escape ovulation, so the study is too small to draw definite conclusions. In another study with a small sampling, 10% of the control group, which didn't miss a pill, experienced escape ovulation, while 28% of those missing two pills ovulated.[102]

J. C. Espinoza, M.D., says,

> Today it is clear that in at least 5% of the cycles of women on the combined Pill "escape ovulation" occurs. This fact means that conception is possible during those cycles, but implantation will be prevented and the "conceptus" (child) will die. That rate is statistically equivalent to one abortion every other year for all women on the Pill.[103]

In a segment from his *Abortion Question and Answers*, published online by Ohio Right to Life, Dr. Jack Willke states:

> The newer low-estrogen pills allow "breakthrough" ovulation in up to 20% or more of the months used. Such a released ovum is fertilized perhaps 10% of the time. These tiny new lives which result, at our present "guesstimations," in 1% to 2% of the pill months, do not survive. The reason is that at one week of life this tiny new boy or girl cannot implant in the womb lining and dies.[104]

There are factors that can increase the rate of breakthrough ovulation and increase the likelihood of the Pill causing an abortion. Dr. Kuhar says,

The abortifacient potential of OCs is further magnified in OC users who concomitantly take certain antibiotics and anticonvulsants, which decrease ovulation suppression effectiveness. It should be noted that antibiotic use among OC users is not uncommon, such women being more susceptible to bacterial, yeast and fungal infections secondary to OC use.[105]

When the first mechanism fails, how often does the second work?

We've seen that various sources and studies put breakthrough ovulation among Pill-takers at rates of 2-10%, 4-10%, 4.7%, 7%, 14%, 10%, and 20%. The next question is, **how many times when ovulation occurs does the second mechanism, the thickened cervical mucus, prevent sperm from reaching the egg?** There is no way to be sure, but while this mechanism certainly works sometimes, it may not work most of the time.

Drs. Chang and Hunt did experiments on rabbits that could not be done on human beings.[106] They gave the rabbits estrogen and progestin to mimic the Pill, then artificially inseminated them. Next, they killed the rabbits and did microscopic studies to examine how many sperm had reached the fallopian tubes and could have fertilized an egg.

Progestin, the hormone that thickens cervical mucus, might be expected to prevent nearly all the sperm from traveling to the tubes. However, it did not. In every rabbit that had taken the progestin, there were still thousands of sperm which reached the fallopian tubes, as many as 72% of the number in the control group. The progestin-caused increase in thickness of cervical mucus did not significantly inhibit sperm from reaching the egg in the rabbit.

This is certainly not definitive proof, since there can be significant physiological differences between animals and humans. However, animals are routinely used for such experiments to determine possible or probable results in humans. Though I have read several studies on human sperm transport, they seemed to offer no helpful information related to this subject. Dr. Melvin Taymor of Harvard Medical School admits, "Sperm transport in women appears to be very complex."[107] The study by Chang and Hunt, while not persuasive in and of itself, at least raises questions about the extent of the contraceptive effectiveness of thickened cervical mucus.

When ovulation takes place, how often will the thickened mucus fail to prevent conception? The answer is certainly "some of the time." It may also be "much of the time," or even "most of the time."

When the second mechanism fails, how often does the third work?

The next question is, in those cases when the second mechanism doesn't work, how often does the significantly altered and less hospitable endometrium caused by the Pill interrupt the pregnancy?

The Ortho Corporation's 1991 annual report estimated 13.9 million U.S. women using oral contraceptives. Now, how often would one expect normally fertile couples of average sexual activity to conceive? Dr. Bogomir Kuhar uses a figure of 25%. This is confirmed by my research. In "Estimates of human fertility and pregnancy loss," Michael J. Zinaman and associates cite a study by Wilcox in which "following 221 couples without known impediments of fertility, [they] observed a per cycle conception rate of 25% over the first three cycles."[108]

Multiplying this by the low 2% ovulation figure among Pill takers, and factoring in a 25% conception rate, Dr. Kuhar arrives at a figure of 834,000 birth-control-pill-induced abortions per year.[109] Multiplying by 10%, a higher estimate of breakthrough ovulation, he states the figure of 4,170,000 abortions per year. (Using other studies, also based on total estimated number of ovulations and U.S. users, Dr. Kuhar attributes 3,825,000 annual abortions to IUDs; 1,200,000 to Depo-Provera; 2,925,000 to Norplant.)

There are several objections to this method of computation. First, it assumes all women taking the Pill, and their partners, have normal fertility rates of 25%, when in fact some women taking the Pill certainly are less fertile than this, as are some of their partners. Second, the computation fails to take into account the Pill's thickening of the cervical mucus which may significantly reduce the rate of conception. Third, it fails to consider the 3% rate of sustained pregnancy each month among Pill-takers, which obviously are not Pill-induced abortions.

Of course, everything depends on the true rate of breakthrough ovulation, and the true rate of contraception due to thickened cervical mucus, both of which remain unknown. Even if the range of abortions is less than indicated by Dr. Kuhar's computation, however, the total numbers could still be very high.

Several medical researchers have assured me scientific studies could be conducted on this. So far, though, the issue of Pill-induced abortions hasn't received attention. Since no conclusive figures exist, we are left with the indirect but substantial evidence of the observably diminished capacity of the Pill-affected endometrium to sustain life. Since there is nothing to indicate otherwise, it seems possible that implantation in the inhospitable endometrium may be the exception rather than the rule. For every child who does implant, many others may not. Of course, we don't know the percentage that will implant even in a *normal* endometrium unaffected by the Pill. **But there is every reason to believe that whatever that percentage is, the Pill significantly lowers it**.

Let's try a different approach to the numbers. According to Pill manufacturers, approximately fourteen million American women take the Pill each year. At the 3% annual sustained pregnancy rate, which is firmly established statistically, in any year there will be 420,000 detected pregnancies of Pill-takers. (I say "detected" pregnancies, since pregnancies that end before implantation will never be detected but are nonetheless real.) Each one of these children has managed to be conceived despite the thickened cervical mucus. Each has managed to implant even in a "hostile" endometrium.

The question is, how many children *failed* to implant in that inhospitable environment who would have implanted in a nurturing environment unhindered by the Pill? The numbers that die might be significantly higher than the numbers that survive. If it were four times as high, that would be 1,680,000 annual deaths; if twice as high, 840,000 deaths. If the same numbers of children do not survive the inhospitable

96

endometrium as do survive, it would be 420,000 deaths. If only half as many died as survived, this would be 210,000; if a quarter as many died as survived 105,000—still a staggering number of Pill-induced abortions each year. Perhaps the figure is even lower than the lowest of these. I certainly hope so. Unfortunately, I have seen no evidence to substantiate my hope.

Even if we believe these fatality numbers are too high, we must avoid the tendency to minimize the value of any human life. I've been told by people, "There's no way six million Jews died in the holocaust. At most it was half a million." My response is, "I think there's reason to believe the figure is much more than half a million. But suppose it *was* a lot less. How many deaths of the innocent does it take to qualify as a tragedy?" Similarly, we might ask, "How many children have to be killed by the Pill to make it too many?"

In his brochure *How the Pill and the IUD Work: Gambling with Life*," Dr. David Sterns asks:

> Just how often does the pill have to rely on this abortive "backup" mechanism? No one can tell you with certainty. Perhaps it is as seldom as 1 to 2% of the time; but perhaps it is as frequently as 50% of the time. Does it matter? The clear conclusion is that it is impossible for any woman on the pill in any given month to know exactly which mechanism is in effect. In other words, **the pill always carries with it the potential to act as an abortifacient**.[110]

Perhaps the annual numbers of Pill-induced abortions add up to millions, perhaps hundreds of thousands, perhaps tens of thousands. When we factor in abortions caused by other birth control chemicals, including the Mini-Pill, Norplant and Depo-Provera, the total figures are almost certainly very high. When prolifers routinely state there are 1.5 million abortions per year in America (I have often said this myself), **we are leaving out all chemical abortions and are therefore vastly understating the true number**. Perhaps we are also immunizing ourselves to the reality that life really does begin at conception and we are morally accountable to act like it.

Let's make this more personal by bringing it down to an individual woman. If a fertile and sexually active woman took the Pill from puberty to menopause, she would have a potential of 390 suppressed ovulations. Eliminating those times when she wouldn't take the Pill because she wanted to have a child, or because she was already pregnant, she might have 330 potentially suppressed ovulations. If 95% of her ovulations were suppressed, this would mean she would have sixteen breakthrough ovulations.

If she is fertile and sexually active, a few of those ovulations might end up in a known pregnancy because the second and third mechanisms both fail. Of the other fourteen ova, perhaps nine would never be fertilized, some prevented by the number two mechanism, the thickened cervical mucus, and some attributable to the normal rate of nonpregnancy. And perhaps, as a result of the number three mechanism, she might have five early abortions because though conception took place, the children could not be implanted in the endometrium.

If the same woman took the Pill for only ten years, she might have one or two abortions instead of five. Again, we don't know the exact figures. Some would say these estimates are too high, but based on my research it appears equally probable they are too low.

There is no way to be certain, but a woman taking the Pill might over time have no Pill-induced abortions, or she might have one, three or a dozen of them.

We have not even taken into account here the other abortive mechanisms of the Pill documented earlier, including the peristalsis within the fallopian tube that decreases the chances of implantation, and the chemical dangers to an already conceived child whose mother unknowingly continues to take the Pill. Neither have we considered the residual effect of the Pill that can inhibit implantation as much as a few months after a woman has stopped using it.

The evidence, not wishful thinking, should govern our beliefs. The numbers have not been decisively determined, and may never be this side of eternity. Based on what we do know, we must ask and answer this question: is it morally right to unnecessarily risk the lives of children by taking the Pill?

Responding to the Evidence:

Questions & Objections

In the process of research I've had countless conversations with fellow Christians, including physicians and pastors. These are the questions and objections people have most often raised.

"If this is true, why haven't we been told?"

There are many possible answers to this question. One is that concerns about abortions, especially early ones, are not widespread among researchers, scientists and the medical community in general. Since preventing implantation isn't of any ethical concern except to those who believe God creates people at the point of conception, it isn't terribly surprising the experts haven't gotten the word out. In their minds, why should they?

Dr. T. B. Woutersz, an employee of Wyeth Laboratories, made an amazing admission about birth control pill studies in his article "A Low-Dose Combination Oral Contraceptive":

> Despite extensive clinical studies conducted by manufacturers of marketed products, only these published papers of study cohorts are available for

the benefit of the prescribing physician. All other published papers represent selected, partial reports of individual investigators. This does not afford a physician much opportunity to make an educated selection of an oral contraceptive.[111]

The individual who brought this to my attention is also a Wyeth employee, who asked not to be identified. In a letter dated August 11, 1997 this person told me, "Many, probably most, birth control studies are not published. They are never published in their entirety. This is a very competitive business. Companies are not obligated to publish proprietary information."

This helps explain why it was so difficult for me to obtain research information from the Pill-manufacturers. They have their own research departments with dozens of full-time researchers who must produce thousands of pages of findings every year. But these findings are distilled down into very small packets of information, including the three operative mechanisms stated in the PDR, the third of which is prevention of implantation. I did not manage to get from any of the manufacturers any detailed studies to confirm exactly how they came to their conclusions. I had to search out on my own the research information in medical journals, which is usually based on much smaller samplings with a great deal less funding behind them.

The published indications of Pill-caused abortions is substantial. But it is spread out in dozens of obscure and technical scientific journals. Consequently, not only is the most significant evidence not in print, but relatively few physicians—and almost no one in the general public—have ever seen the most compelling evidence that *is* in print. If they have heard anything at all, it has only been piecemeal. The evidence that has managed to make it to publication has fallen through the cracks and failed to get the attention of physicians.

Many well-meaning physicians, including Christians, and including Ob/GYNs and Family Practitioners, simply are not aware of this evidence. I know this, because that's exactly what a number of them have told me. This is not entirely surprising. Consider the staggering amount of medical knowledge that currently exists. Now picture the average physician who is both conscientious and overworked, swamped with patients. He might read medical journals in an area of special interest, but there is no way any human being can be fully appraised of the tens of thousands of medical studies conducted each year in this country.

When patients hear someone suggest the Pill causes abortions, they will often come to their physician, who may be prolife, and ask if this is true. The physician may sincerely say, "According to my understanding, the Pill just prevents conception, it doesn't cause abortions. You have nothing to be concerned about."

Most physicians assume that if the Pill really caused abortions, they would surely know it. In most cases they are not deliberately misleading their patients. Unfortunately, the bottom line is that their patients do end up misled. Based on their physician's reassurances, they don't look into the matter further— nor would most know where to look even if they wanted to. In reality, the dedicated physician is extremely busy and confident that the Pill only prevents conception; typically he too does not take the time to do the necessary research.

An isolated reference here or there simply isn't sufficient to change or even challenge the deeply ingrained pro-Pill consensus of medicine, society or the church. If *Time* magazine devoted a cover story to the subject, the information would reach a popular level in a way it never has before. But *Time* and most of its readers would have little interest in the subject. Perhaps eventually a major Christian magazine will present this research to the people who should care the most. So far this has not happened.

Medical semantics have also played a critical role in obscuring the Pill's abortive mechanism. As documented earlier in this book, in 1976 the word "contraceptive" was redefined by the American College of Obstetricians and Gynecologists (ACOG), to include agents that prevent implantation. Changes in terminology typically occur to draw more careful scientific distinctions, whereas this one served only to blur the distinction between two clearly separate things, fertilization and implantation. Several prolife Ob/GYNs told me they are convinced this move, happening three years after the Supreme Court's 1973 legalization of abortion, was a deliberate attempt to obscure concerns about birth control chemicals that sometimes cause early abortions.

Because of the semantic change, medical professionals can honestly say that the Pill is only a contraceptive, even if they know it sometimes acts to prevent implantation. For example, Dr. Linda J. Martin wrote to *Pediatric News* pointing out that while an August 1997 article had claimed the emergency contraception pill could "prevent up to 800,000 abortions a year," exactly the opposite was the case——"they would in fact cause 800,000 abortions a year."

Her logic was that life begins at conception, not implantation. The physician who wrote the article, Dr. James Trussel, responded, "Both the National Institutes of Health and the American College of Obstetricians and Gynecologists define pregnancy as beginning with implantation. Therefore, emergency contraceptive pills are not abortifacient."[112]

This is a dramatic but increasingly common example of semantic depersonalization—using an arbitrary redefinition to relegate a child to nonexistence. What might properly be called a "contraimplantive" mechanism is called instead a "contraceptive" mechanism. An article on 'morning after' pills explains that they are "ordinary birth control pills containing the hormones estrogen and progestin, but are taken in a higher dose up to 72 hours after unprotected intercourse."[113] The article explains that the pills prevent implantation, but the large font pull quote from Dr. Jack Leversee of the University of Washington School of Medicine assures readers, "We are not doing away with a pregnancy; we are preventing it from ever becoming a pregnancy."

Undiscerning prolifers may read such statements and be reassured that these pills don't cause abortions. Attaching new meanings to old words such as conception and pregnancy has succeeded in making it sound like the Pill and other hormonal contraceptives don't kill human beings. It has done nothing, however, to change the fact that sometimes that's exactly what they do.

Even when the information about the Pill rises to the surface here and there, so many Christians— including pastors and parachurch leaders—have used and recommended the Pill, that we have a natural resistance to raising this issue or looking into it seriously when others raise it. (I know this from my own experience.) This is likely why so few individuals or organizations have researched or drawn attention to this subject. Among other things, organizations fear a loss of financial support from donors who would object to criticism of the Pill.

We also cannot escape the fact that the Pill is a multi-billion dollar worldwide industry. Its manufacturers, the drug companies, have tremendous vested interests. So do many physicians prescribing it. I do *not* mean by this that most physicians prescribe it primarily for financial gain; I do mean it is a significant part of the total income of many practices.

An appendix in *The Woman's Complete Guide to Personal Health Care*, by Debra Evans,[114] is entitled "A Physician Looks at Doctors' and Pharmacists' Profits from Prescribing Birth Control Pills." The writer carefully calculates the costs of various procedures and comes up with a cost summary per patient. Added to this is the fact that each woman with a family will take her children to the family practitioner who prescribes her contraceptives, and usually her husband will go to that doctor. Using averages for frequency of visits, and factoring in word of mouth or patient-to-patient referral, the writer calculates that income linked to patients for whom the doctor prescribes birth control pills range from 55 to 74% of his total income.

Because of the Pill's popularity, physicians who stop prescribing it will likely lose many patients and their families to other doctors. Even many prolife physicians resist the notion that the Pill causes abortions and are unlikely to change their position or even share with their patients evidence such as that presented in this book. (Thankfully, there are certainly exceptions to this.)

Those in the best place to disseminate this information are the Pill-manufacturers. The problem, however, is that they gain customers by convincing them the Pill works, *not* by teaching them exactly how it works. No one takes the Pill because she knows it prevents implantation. But some, perhaps many, might stop taking it if they knew it does.

Hence, a pharmaceutical company has nothing to gain by drawing attention to this information, and potentially a great deal to lose. There are many people in America who profess to believe life begins at conception, and companies do not want these people to stop using their pills. This concern for good public relations was exceedingly evident to me in my conversations with staff members at four major Pill manufacturers. It is also demonstrated in the fact that their FDA-monitored disclosures in the fine-print professional labeling and in the *Physician's Desk Reference* all mention that the Pill prevents implantation, but very few of their package inserts and none of their colorful consumer booklets say anything about it.

Dr. James Walker, in his paper "Oral Contraception: A Different Perspective," points out the Pill's potential to cause abortion. He then says,

> A large percentage of consumers would undoubtedly refuse to use this form of birth control if they were aware that oral contraceptives worked in this way. Also, a large number of physicians would refrain from using this method of contraception if they were aware

of the abortifacient mechanism of oral contraceptives...why is the medical (or prescribing) and consumer population so poorly informed? It could be that the pharmaceutical industry is interested in making large profits without regard for the sanctity of human life. Or it could be that the medical community has become so conditioned to supply means for instant gratification, that our eyes have been blinded to the eternal consequences of our daily action.[115]

On the most basic level, the widespread ignorance and blindness on this issue among Christians may be largely attributable to supernatural forces of evil which promote the deaths of the innocent while lying and misleading to cover those deaths. (I will address this in the Conclusion.)

"I don't trust this evidence."

One physician told me that he thinks the evidence I've cited is simply incorrect. He said, "I don't trust these medical studies. I just don't think they're accurate."

I asked him if he had any objective reason for his distrust. He cited the study I dealt with earlier concerning Norplant. Since he said he didn't trust dozens of medical sources connecting the Pill with prevention of implantation, I asked him why he trusted a single source not even dealing with the Pill, while rejecting those sources offering evidence to the contrary.

This illustrates a tendency we all have, but which we should all resist—the tendency to believe whatever we can use to defend our position, and to disbelieve whatever contradicts our position. We must be willing to seriously examine evidence that goes against the grain of what we believe, so that rather than reading our position into the evidence, we allow the evidence to determine our position.

The same physician, a committed prolife advocate, wrote to me that breast-feeding results in "an atrophic thin endometrium." He then stated, "So, in theory, if you state oral contraceptives may cause an abortion, logically the same could be said for breast-feeding." He told me that, to be consistent, if I was going to call the Pill an abortifacient I would have to say the same of breast-feeding.

I submitted this argument to another Ob/Gyn, Dr. Paul Hayes. In a August 15, 1997 email Dr. Hayes responded,

> It is an erroneous misuse of words to say that breast-feeding creates an atrophic endometrium. Lack of ovulation during breast-feeding accounts for a state of the endometrium that is *inactive*, precisely because no ovulation is taking place. This is unlike the Pill where ovulation can take place…but the effect of the progestin is to make an *atrophic* lining, inhibiting nidation. There is no comparison between the two.[116]

"If we don't know how often abortions happen, why *shouldn't* we take the Pill?"

How are we as Christians to make ethical decisions in the absence of scientifically incontrovertible proof that the Pill causes abortion at least some of the time? In light of the fact that we have very substantial evidence (I believe most unbiased researchers would say overwhelming evidence) but not absolute proof the

Pill can cause abortions, as Christians who agree that we do not have the right to take a child's life, is It ethical to prescribe or use the Pill?

Dr. Walter Larimore addresses this issue in an excellent article published in *Ethics and Medicine* journal. He says that in a climate in which there is legitimate debate, opponents of the Pill argue that "a moral birth control method must be exclusively contraceptive; e.g., it must (1) work exclusively...by preventing conception from occurring and (2) cause no harm to the conceived child."[117] Since the Pill *may* cause early abortions, whether a small or a large number, it should not be used.

On the other side, defenders argue that the Pill may *not* cause abortions, and since it may not, we should feel free to use and prescribe it. Some also say that *if* the Pill causes abortions, these are only "mini-abortions" which occur "prior to or just following implantation."[118] They therefore suggest that there is no ethical dilemma to be resolved. (This would be true, of course, only if human life does not begin at conception, but at implantation—a contention for which many of us believe there is no logical, scientific or biblical evidence.)

In my experience, all but the most hard-core defenders of the Pill—and only prolife defenders, since prochoice defenders invariably recognize the Pill can prevent implantation—will acknowledge that it can cause at least a small number of abortions. The moral question, then, is this: since we are uncertain about how many abortions it causes, how should we act in light of our uncertainty?

In teaching college ethics courses, I have framed the question this way: If a hunter is uncertain whether the movement in the brush is caused by a deer or a person, should his uncertainty lead him to shoot or not shoot?

If you're driving at night and you think the dark figure ahead on the road may be a child, but it may just be the shadow of a tree, do you drive into it or do you put on the brakes? What if you think there's a 50% chance it's a child? 30% chance? 10% chance? 1% chance? How certain do you have to be that you may kill a child before you should modify your preferred action (to not put on your brakes) and resort to putting on your brakes?

My question is this: *shouldn't we give the benefit of the doubt to life?* Let's say that you are skeptical of all this research, all these studies, all these medical textbooks and journal articles, and all the Pill manufacturers' clear statements that the Pill sometimes prevents implantation (and therefore results in the death of a child). You might ask yourself if the reason for your skepticism is your personal bias and vested interests. But let's assume you are genuinely uncertain. Is it a Christlike attitude to say "Because taking the Pill may or may not kill a child, I will therefore take or prescribe the Pill"? If we are uncertain, shouldn't we take the ethical high ground by saying our uncertainty should compel us *not* to take or prescribe the Pill?

My research has convinced me the evidence is compelling. It is only the numbers that are uncertain. Can we really say in good conscience, "Because I'm uncertain exactly how *many* children are killed by the

Pill, therefore I will take or prescribe it"? How many dead children would it take to be too many?

It seems to me more Christlike to say, "Because the evidence indicates the Pill can sometimes causes abortions, I will not use or prescribe it and will seek to inform others of its dangers to unborn children."

"Spontaneous miscarriages are common—early abortions aren't that big a deal."

One physician pointed out to me that there are many spontaneous abortions and miscarriages. Because of this, he felt we should not be troubled by pre-implantation abortions caused by the Pill. They are just some among many.

I've heard the same logic used to defend fertility research and in-vitro fertilization in which embryos are conceived outside the womb. Three to six of these may be implanted in a uterus in the hopes one may live, but the majority die, and some are frozen or discarded. In the best-case scenario, two to five die in the attempt to implant one, and often all of them die.

When, even under optimal conditions, physicians attempt to implant an embryo conceived in-vitro, it is true that there is a low success rate. According to Dr. Leon Speroff, the success rate in any given cycle is 13.5% and since typically three to six embryos may be used to attempt implantation, the actual survival rate is just over 3%. This means that 29 out of 30 embryos die in the attempt to implant a child.[119]

In-vitro fertilization implantation data is not applicable to natural implantation. Concerning the latter, as documented in their book *Conception to Birth*, Drs. Kline, Stein and Susser put forward certain assumptions then state,

> ...the preimplantation data would indicate that at least 50 per cent of all fertilizations will not result in a live birth...the probability of loss in the interval between the preimplantation and postimplantation periods alone is 30 per cent.[120]

In their article "Estimates of human fertility and pregnancy loss," Michael J. Zinaman and associates cite different studies showing spontaneous abortion rates of 15% to 20%, 13% to 22%, 12 to 14%, and 20-62%.[121]

This confirms that there are in fact many early miscarriages. Since this is true, however, does it therefore follow, "Because God permits—or nature causes—millions of spontaneous abortions each year, it's okay if we cause some too"?

There is a big difference, a cosmic difference, between God and us! What God is free to do and what we are free to do are not the same. God is the giver and taker of life. God is the potter; we are the clay (Isaiah 45:9-11). His prerogatives are unique to Him. He is the Creator; we are the creatures. *He* has the right to take human life, but *we* do not. (See ***Appendix D:* God is Creator and Owner of all people**.)

Nature is under the curse of sin and as a result there is widespread death in this world, both inside and outside the womb (Romans 8:19-22). God is the

Superintendent of nature and can overrule it when he so chooses. But none of this permits us to say, "Because God lets so many people die, I'll go ahead and kill some of them myself." **Spontaneous abortions of women not taking contraceptives are not our responsibility. Abortions caused by contraceptives we choose to take and prescribe are.**

The same principle applies when someone concludes that since a baby will probably die within a few days or weeks of his birth, we may as well abort him now. The difference is between losing a child to death, by God's sovereign choice, and our choosing to kill that child. This is a fundamental and *radical* difference. (See **Appendix E: God has exclusive prerogatives over human life and death**.)

I have several letters from Christian physicians and organizations that use the term "micro-abortion" in reference to the possibility that the Pill prevents implantation. Such semantics minimize the abortion, as if it isn't "real" or important like surgical abortions of bigger children. We should avoid such dehumanizing terms. Though the child is very small the child is still a child and therefore the abortion is just as big in its importance.

Just because many children die very young doesn't make their deaths insignificant. True, we may lose several children we don't even know about, through early spontaneous miscarriages. But that in no way justifies choosing to take something into our bodies that puts other children at risk.

"Taking the Pill means fewer children die in spontaneous abortions."

A letter from one Christian organization (which I prefer not to name) says this:

> It has been pointed out that a woman who is not taking birth control pills is actually more likely to experience the loss of an embryo—some studies indicate that up to 80% of conceived embryos naturally fail to implant—than one who is on the pill, which rarely, if ever, permits conception.

The logic seems to be that when we use a chemical that kills some children we can take consolation in knowing that this same chemical prevents many other children from ever being conceived and therefore from ever dying. This is convoluted logic, and again it puts us in the place of God.

If there are fewer miscarriages because of the Pill it is not because the Pill brings any benefit to a preborn child, but only because it results in fewer children conceived. This is an illusion—it's not that lives are being preserved but simply that there are fewer lives to preserve. There is less death only because there is less life.

Using this logic, the most prolife thing we could do would be to eliminate all pregnancy. We could then congratulate ourselves that we also eliminated abortion. In the process, of course, we will have eliminated children. Similarly, reducing the number of people in society could lower the number of people with cancer. But we would hardly think of that as a cure—especially if the means we used to have less people involved killing some of them.

"Without the Pill there would be more elective abortions."

A prolife physician pointed out in a letter to her pastor that 50% of unwanted pregnancies end in abortion. Therefore a million more unwanted pregnancies each year could mean a half million more abortions each year. In other words, the logic is it's better to use the most effective birth control means possible even if it does cause abortions, because if it isn't used there will be even more.

Suppose for a moment this were true. What is the logic? "Let's go ahead and take action that will kill some children now because at least if we do there may be other children, more of them, who won't get killed." The same approach could be used to deny drowning children access to a crowded life raft. This sort of pragmatism rings hollow when we put certain human lives at risk, without their consent, for the supposed good of others.

Ultimately, however, the premise is not true, since unfortunately it is only a small minority who would even consider not taking the Pill because it causes early abortions. The only people who will stop taking the Pill for this reason are not only prolife, but deeply committed to their beliefs. This book won't have much if any impact in the secular world. I do hope it will encourage some of God's people to live by a higher moral code than the world does.

A person who as a matter of conscience will not risk the life of a newly-conceived child—whose presence in her womb she can't even yet feel—will surely not turn around and kill a child just because she has an unplanned pregnancy. Among people who stop taking the Pill to protect unborn children, there may be more unplanned pregnancies, but they will result in births, not abortions.

"Pill-takers don't *intend* to have abortions."

I've frequently been told that because most people's intention in taking the Pill is to prevent conception, not to have an abortion, it's therefore ethical for them to continue taking the Pill.

I certainly agree most women taking the Pill don't intend to get abortions. In fact, I'm convinced 99% of them are unaware this is even possible. (Which is a sad commentary on the lack of informed consent by Pill-takers.) But the fact remains that while the *intentions* of those taking the Pill may be harmless, the *results* can be just as fatal.

A nurse giving your child an injection could sincerely intend no harm to your child, but if she unknowingly injects him with a fatal poison, her good intentions will not lessen the tragedy. Whether the nurse has the heart of a murderer or a saint, your child is equally dead. The best intentions do nothing to reverse the most disastrous results.

In this sense, taking the Pill is analogous to playing Russian roulette, but with more chambers and therefore less risk per episode. In Russian roulette, participants usually don't *intend* to shoot themselves. Their intention is irrelevant, however, because if they play the game long enough they just can't beat the odds. Eventually they die.

The Russian roulette of the Pill is done with someone else's life. Each time someone taking the Pill engages in sex, she runs the risk of aborting a child. Instead of a one in six chance, maybe it's a one in thirty or one in a hundred or one in five hundred chance; I'm not sure. I am sure that it's a real risk—the scientific evidence tells us the chemical "gun" is loaded. The fact that she will not know when a child has been aborted in no way changes whether or not a child *is* aborted. Every month she continues to take the Pill increases her chances of having her first—or next—silent abortion. She could have one, two, a half dozen or a dozen of these without ever having a clue.

A prolife physician told me he felt comfortable still prescribing the Pill because "It's *primarily* contraceptive and only *secondarily* abortive."

Suppose a friend gave you a bottle of diet pills and said, "Their primary effect is to suppress your appetite, and cause you to lose weight." You say, "But I've heard they can cause major problems." Your friend tells you, "True, they can result in heart attacks, blindness and kidney failures, but don't worry about that; those are only secondary effects, not primary."

The point is, even if it doesn't happen most of the time, whenever an effect *does* happen it is not secondary in importance, it is primary. Even if the Pill doesn't usually cause an abortion, whenever it does it is just as real an abortion as if that were its primary effect.

"Why not just use high estrogen pills?"

One physician said to me, "Pill manufacturers have never been sued by an unborn child who dies, but they have been sued by many women suffering from the serious side effects of high estrogen. For liability reasons alone, they will never go back to making high dose estrogen pills."

Even when pills had mega doses of estrogen, however, the annual pregnancy rate of women on the Pill was still 1% and the effects on thinning the endometrium were comparable to what they are now. This means that breakthrough ovulations certainly still took place, even if at a lower rate. It may have added up to *fewer* abortions then, but not *no* abortions.

I asked pharmacist Richard Hill at Ortho-McNeil if the higher dose pills were more successful in suppressing ovulation. He said, "Not really—there's a ceiling point of estrogen, beyond which more isn't better. By the time you get to 35 micrograms, for most people you've reached the point of maximum ovulation suppression." (This may contradict some other sources I cited earlier. I include it for the sake of representing different viewpoints.)

In any case, unless you were able to get three current "high dose" birth control prescriptions of 50 micrograms each and take three pills a day, you could not equal the 1960's *standard* dose of 150 micrograms of estrogen.

Even if you did, you would have to face the very serious side effects and risks to a woman's health that motivated pill manufacturers to lower the estrogen level in the first place. In light of these dangers, it's virtually certain no physician would give such a prescription. It would probably be unwise to take it if he did.

"You can't avoid every risk."

We put our children and ourselves at risk every time we drive a car. If we let our kids go swimming we take risks. Our child's ability to grow, mature and gain confidence—and trust in God— in a world of risks partially depends on our willingness to take reasonable risks with them.

But we are also careful not to take unnecessary risks. Our risks are wise and calculated. Because we love our children we expose them only to a measured level of risk—they ride in the car, yes, but we belt them in and drive carefully. As they grow up they learn to make their own decisions as to what level of risk is wise and acceptable.

The younger our children are, the less risks we take with them. We might leave an eight-year-old free to roam the house, while we wouldn't a toddler. When we are talking about a newly conceived human being, if we take the Pill it is his *life* we are risking. ***The reason we're doing so is not for his growth and maturity, but for our convenience.*** We are unnecessarily putting him at risk of his very survival. Through the choice to take certain chemicals into our bodies via the Pill, we may be robbing him of the single most important thing we can offer a newly-conceived child—a hospitable environment in which he can be nourished and grow.

We would not consider withholding food and a home and physical safety for our children who are already born. We would not be careless about what we eat and drink and the chemicals we ingest and the activities we do that could jeopardize our preborn child six months after conception. Then neither should we put our child at unnecessary risk six *days* after conception. Yes, we can't know for certain our child is even there at six days. But if we've been sexually active we know she *may* be there. And therefore we should do nothing that could unnecessarily jeopardize her life.

A sexually active woman runs a new risk of aborting a child with every Pill she takes. Of course, the decision to take the Pill isn't just a woman's but her husband's, and he is every bit as responsible for the choice as she is. As the God-appointed leader in the home, in fact, he may be even more responsible.

How much risk is acceptable risk? Part of it depends on the alternatives. There is no such thing as a car or a house that poses *no* risk to your children. But there is such a thing as a contraceptive method that does not put a child's life at risk. There *are* safe alternatives to the Pill that do not and cannot cause abortions.

No matter what level of risk parents decide to take with their children, surely we should agree that they deserve to know if evidence indicates they are taking such a risk. To be aware of the evidence that taking the Pill may cause abortions and not to share that information with parents is to keep them in the dark and rob them of exercising an informed choice about their own children.

"How can we practice birth control without the Pill?"

I am now treading on ground that is bound to offend Christians on both sides of the contraceptive debate. Many, as my wife and I did for years, will have used contraceptives, believing this is acceptable to God. Others do not believe this. They would respond to this question not by pointing to alternative methods of birth control, but by saying, "We shouldn't be taking birth control in the first place—it is God who opens and closes the womb, and it's playing God to try to dictate your family size. The Bible says children are a blessing from the Lord, not inconveniences to be avoided. Children are blessings sent from God. Which of his other blessings—such as financial provision, a good job, a strong marriage, or a solid church—are you desperately trying to avoid?"

On the one hand, for various reasons my wife and I used birth control and "stopped" after two children. If we had it to do over again, would we do it differently? I honestly don't know, though I am certain we would give it more Bible study, thought and prayer before making our decision. As I tell the students in my Bible college ethics class, I think we must look at both sides of this issue seriously. Certainly, we must be sure we are not succumbing to our society's "Planned Parenthood" view of children rather than God's view of children. (See *Appendix G:* **How God Sees Children.)**

Regardless of our position on contraceptives, I think we should be able to agree that God is grieved by the anti-child mentality that surfaces sometimes even in the church, where snide remarks are made to and about families with more than three children and cold stares are the response to every crying baby. Whether someone has a large family or a small family (like we do), I believe large families should be seen not as the products of irresponsibility, but as blessings from God. My own father was the tenth of thirteen children. Am I glad his parents didn't stop after nine children? Of course I am. If they would have, I wouldn't be here, and neither would my daughters—and they wouldn't be making the great difference for Christ they're making.

However, this book is *not* motivated by a desire to persuade people that all attempts at family planning are wrong. I have only one agenda here and it is not a hidden one. My position is one I believe all Christians should agree on regardless of their differing positions on family planning. That position is this: **no family planning which sacrifices the lives of a family member can be morally right and pleasing to God**.

For genuinely prolife Christians who believe in family planning and the use of contraceptives, the question is, "what are the non-abortive alternatives to the Pill, Minipill, IUD, Depo-Provera and Norplant?" The fact is, there are effective, non-abortifacient alternatives to the Pill. One answer may be the barrier methods, such as condoms and diaphragms. There are also spermicides, which come in creams, jellies and foams, as well as "films," which are thin squares. Though they can cause problems and inconveniences of their own, such as allergic reactions, none of these are abortive.

Someone said there is evidence latex can be toxic and therefore they believe it's possible the regular use of condoms can have abortive effects. I have seen no scientific evidence linking condoms to abortions, and therefore do not oppose them on this basis. (Latex is most common, but not the only option; some condoms are made of polyurethane and others of animal tissue.)

I have not seen evidence that diaphragms or spermicides are anything but contraceptives. Regardless of other concerns about them—and we should certainly investigate the possible side effects of anything we put in our bodies—they appear not to cause abortions. (One reader pointed out, however, that if spermicides kill sperm so effectively, it's possible they could be harmful to a conceived child. Again, I'm currently unaware of any evidence this is true.)

A source of information on nonabortive contraceptives is located on the Internet at www.epigee.org/guide. Assembled by a woman who works in a pregnancy care center, this site explains human reproduction and conception, and then deals specifically with the nature and effectiveness of male and female condoms, spermicides, diaphragms, cervical cap, lactation, electronic fertility indicator, and Natural Family Planning (often abbreviated simply as "NFP").

"Natural Family Planning" is *not* simply the old calendar "rhythm" method, which was based on biological averages but was not effective for women with irregular cycles. Rather, it is a very thoughtful and scientific approach, based on the fact that during each menstrual cycle a woman becomes fertile and

123

then naturally infertile, and there are physical signs to indicate these fertile and infertile times. The Sympto-Thermal method crosschecks mucus and temperature indicators in a way that is highly accurate and reliable.

The Couple to Couple League defines Natural Family Planning as "the practice of achieving or avoiding pregnancies according to an informed awareness of a woman's fertility."[122] They cite studies showing their methods to be extremely effective. They certainly are safe, as they do not involve taking any chemicals or implanting any devices.

Natural Family Planning classes and home study courses are available to teach couples how the process works. You may contact the following organizations for information: Couple to Couple League, 513-471-2000, www.ccli.org, ccli@ccli.org; BOMA-USA (Billings Ovulation Method Association), 320-252-2100, www.woomb.org, sek@gw.stcdio.org; The Creighton Model, www.creightonmodel.com, popepaul@mitec.net; or www.bioself.ch. Though I'm not intimately familiar with these methods, what I've seen suggests they're worth exploring.

Some will respond, "But these methods aren't as effective—we may have an unwanted child." In fact, the barrier methods, especially when used in combination with spermicides, can be highly effective. True, they are not as effective as the Pill and certainly less convenient. Natural Family Planning, practiced by informed couples, can be just as effective as the Pill. Some studies suggest it is actually *more* effective, with a 99% success rate. These studies are cited by materials from the Couple to Couple League, as well as those of the American Life League (P.O.

Box 1350, Stafford, Virginia 22555; 703-659-4171; www.all.org).

But let's look at the "worst case" scenario of a Christian couple not taking the Pill—conceiving and giving birth to an unplanned child. Consider how many people whose children were unplanned have been richly blessed. These are not "accidents," they are precious creations of God. Babies are not cancerous tumors to be desperately avoided and removed. That they are unplanned by us does not mean they are unplanned by God.

We have to weigh the increased "risk" of having a child, a person God calls a blessing, against the possibility of killing a child, an act God calls an abomination. No matter where a Christian stands on the birth control issue, we should surely be able to agree that *the possibility of having a child is always better than the possibility of killing a child*.

Many unwanted pregnancies have resulted in wanted children. I know a man whose married daughter recently stopped taking the Pill when she learned it sometimes causes abortion. She got pregnant soon thereafter. It didn't fit this couple's plan, but now they're thrilled to have this child. The grandfather said to me with a smile, "thanks to my daughter not taking the Pill, God gave us a wonderful grandchild!" Is that really so bad? Though I am not arguing against birth control per se, I am convinced God was pleased by this couple's choice to not place children at risk for the sake of their preferences and convenience. That he has chosen to give them a child may be a challenge, but he should not be regarded as a curse, but a blessing.

There may also be some health benefits to women who choose not to take the Pill. As anyone who has read the inserts packaged with birth control pills knows, there are serious risks to some women associated with oral contraceptives, including increased incidence of blood clots, strokes, heart attacks, high blood pressure, sexually transmitted diseases, pelvic inflammatory disease, infertility, breast cancer, cervical cancer, liver tumors, and ectopic pregnancy. These and other risks are spelled out under each BCP listing in the *Physician's Desk Reference*. The health issue is *not* my central concern in this book, but it is certainly worth considering.

There are some benefits in taking the Pill that have no relation to issues of pregnancy. Doctors prescribe it to regulate hormones connected to conditions such as ovarian cysts. Among many other uses, it is prescribed to get women "on schedule" who desire ultimately to go off the Pill and have children. If one was careful to use a nonabortive contraceptive in addition to the Pill, it might be reasonable to use the Pill briefly to regulate her periods in preparation for a pregnancy. If a single woman who is not sexually active has had certain ovarian problems, her doctor's prescription of the Pill to treat her condition might be very appropriate.

As long as sexually inactive women are aware of the physical risks to themselves, which they may well determine to be acceptable, they should feel free to take the Pill for its other benefits. The moral problem is when, regardless of the reasons for taking it, a sexually active woman takes the Pill and thereby runs the continuous risk of aborting a child.

"I never knew this— should I feel guilty?"

I know *exactly* what you're experiencing. If we had known this, Nanci and I would never have used the Pill. But we didn't know, and there's nothing we can do now to change that. If we were still using the Pill, upon discovering these realities, we would immediately stop using it. But I also must deal with my failure in recent years, long after we stopped using the Pill, to investigate the occasional reference I heard to the possibility that the Pill causes abortions.

What about guilt? There is true guilt and there are guilt feelings. The latter often plague us even when we are not guilty, or *no longer guilty* because we have confessed and Christ has forgiven us. Whenever we have done something in ignorance, it is hard to discern our level of responsibility, but Scripture makes clear we are capable of doing wrong even when not consciously aware of it.

> When a person commits a violation and sins unintentionally in regard to any of the LORD's holy things, he is to bring to the LORD as a penalty a ram from the flock…It is a guilt offering…If a person sins and does what is forbidden in any of the LORD's commands, even though he does not know it, he is guilty and will be held responsible. He is to bring to the priest as a guilt offering a ram from the flock, one without defect…In this way the priest will make atonement for him for the wrong he has committed unintentionally, and he will be forgiven. (Leviticus 5:14-18)

We are to seek out before the Lord and come to terms with unintentional and unknown sins:

127

"How many wrongs and sins have I committed? Show me my offense and my sin." (Job 13:23)

"Who can discern his errors? Forgive my hidden faults." (Psalm 19:12)

"Test me, O LORD, and try me, examine my heart and my mind." (Psalm 26:2)

"I have considered my ways and have turned my steps to your statutes." (Psalm 119:59)

"Search me, O God, and know my heart; test me and know my anxious thoughts. See if there is any offensive way in me, and lead me in the way everlasting." (Psalm 139:23-24)

Scripture clearly teaches we will each stand before the judgment seat of Christ and give an account of what we have done in our lives on earth (Romans 14:10; 2 Corinthians 5:10). While our salvation doesn't depend on our doing things that are honoring to God, our rewards do.

The Bible teaches that by coming to terms now with our sin and our responsibility, we can to a certain extent preserve ourselves from having to face judgment later: "But if we judged ourselves, we would not come under judgment" (1 Corinthians 11:31).

All of us who have used the Pill may have unknowingly caused abortions, and we certainly ran the risk of doing so. All of us who have recommended it are also accountable.

Because of the work of Jesus Christ on the cross on our behalf, God freely offers us pardon and forgiveness for everything—known sins, unknown sins, and actions taken in ignorance and sincerity that may have terrible and unintended results.

> He does not treat us as our sins deserve or repay us according to our iniquities. For as high as the heavens are above the earth, so great is his love for those who fear him; as far as the east is from the west, so far has he removed our transgressions from us. As a father has compassion on his children, so the LORD has compassion on those who fear him; for he knows how we are formed, he remembers that we are dust. (Psalm 103:10-14)

> Who is a God like you, who pardons sin and forgives the transgression of the remnant of his inheritance? You do not stay angry forever but delight to show mercy. You will again have compassion on us; you will tread our sins underfoot and hurl all our iniquities into the depths of the sea. (Micah 7:18-19)

> If we confess our sins, he is faithful and just and will forgive us our sins and purify us from all unrighteousness. (1 John 1:9)

To be honest, I haven't known exactly how to respond to our years of using the Pill, and my recommending it to couples in premarital counseling. My prayer has been something like this—"Lord, I'd like to think this wasn't a sin, given our ignorance. But based on your Word I suspect it probably was. Since I am usually *more* guilty than I think, not less, I should assume I have sinned rather than presuming I have not. Please forgive me. I thank you that the price you paid means I need not labor under the guilt of my wrong choices in the past. Help me *now* to demonstrate the condition of my heart by living out consistently my convictions about the sanctity of human life you have created. Help me never to dare play God by usurping your sole prerogatives as the giver and taker of life. And help me do what I can to encourage my brothers and sisters not to do so either."

I believe in light of our knowledge that the Pill can cause abortions, we should no longer use or recommend it, and should take the opportunity to explain, especially to our brothers and sisters in Christ, why we cannot.

> "Let us examine our ways and test them, and let us return to the LORD." (Lamentations 3:40)

> "He who conceals his sins does not prosper, but whoever confesses and renounces them finds mercy." (Proverbs 28:13)

"We shouldn't lay guilt on people by talking about this."

Someone forwarded to me an email from a Christian physician who is also a Marriage and Family Therapist. Here was his response to this book:

> This will do more harm than good… My overall emotional reaction is one of anger. My intellectual reaction is that this material will have a detrimental impact on good devout Christian couples. It appears to be an example of black or white thinking in an area full of all kinds of shades of gray. The Bible passage that comes to mind is Jesus' comment in Luke 11:46: 'And you experts in the law, woe to you, because you load people down with burdens they can hardly carry.'

A significant part of my work as a therapist for Christians involves helping them overcome the after-effects of religious or spiritual abuse perpetrated by overzealous or misguided religiously motivated individuals. I see this booklet as an example of legalism based on poor science and lack of emotional understanding and compassion.[123]

Interestingly, the writer included no evidence of poor science in this book, nor did he offer any good science to refute it. He appears to assume that one cannot set forth truthful evidence in this arena without being guilty of legalism or spiritual abuse. Unfortunately, I believe this therapist doesn't give either truth or people enough credit. Is truth devoid of grace? Are Christians incapable of handling difficult information or accepting God's provision for guilt? Is it compassionate to hold back disturbing truth from people rather than share it with them so they can make their own choice as to what to believe and seek the Lord's guidance how to respond? It may appear compassionate on its face, but in fact I believe it is paternalistic and condescending.

Many others have told me that it would be better to be silent, to not raise the issue of the Pill's ability to cause abortions. Why? Because it will make people feel guilty. And that is supposedly unkind.

Sometimes, however, a greater sense of guilt and accountability is exactly what we need, for then we can deal with sin in God's way, and be relieved of it rather than ignoring or stuffing it. The same "don't make people feel guilty" logic prompts people not to say what the Bible really says. But ultimately it is never in people's best interests to keep them in ignorance and give them no opportunity to respond to the Lord.

Our mission must be to tell the truth, not to hide it. We are here not simply to help each other *feel* good, but to help each other *be* good. Ultimately, the greatest kindness we can offer each other is the truth. The Christian life is not based on avoiding the truth but on hearing it and submitting to it.

Scripture speaks of a sorrow that leads to repentance (2 Corinthians 7:9). It is far better to feel guilty, repent and become obedient than not to feel guilty, and continue to disobey our Lord, endanger the lives of the innocent, and lay up judgment for ourselves. The right way to no longer feel guilty is to lay our guilt at the foot of the cross, not hide or deny it. The time to take responsibility for our actions is now, not later at the judgment seat of Christ.

I believe this truth-centered approach, communicated with grace, is not only right but ultimately compassionate.

"We shouldn't tell people the Pill may cause abortions because then they'll be held accountable."

I've had it said to me that as long as people don't know the Pill causes abortions, they're better off. If they do hear the truth and don't stop taking the Pill, one woman told me, by giving them this information I've made them more accountable, increased their guilt, and thereby done them a disservice.

Leviticus 5 and other passages dealing with unintentional and unknown sins fly in the face of this "ignorance is bliss" theology. The concept "if we don't know, we're not held accountable" isn't biblical. If it were true, it could be used to justify failing to warn people about sexual immorality, murder, or any other sin. It could be used to claim heathens are better off never hearing the gospel, because then they wouldn't be held accountable for rejecting it.

While it's true we take greater judgment on ourselves by rejecting truth that has been clearly presented, we will also be judged for what we haven't been told but is nonetheless true. It's not for us to withhold truth from our brothers and sisters because we think they won't listen. It's our sacred responsibility to speak up and try to persuade them, and hope and pray they'll listen. Furthermore, *we* will be held accountable for whether or not we've obeyed God by telling them the truth and giving them a chance to respond (Ezekiel 33:1-9).

Even the secular world recognizes it's an ethical mandate that physicians not withhold pertinent information from patients. A physician, pastor or anyone in an authoritative or guiding role might personally choose to take whatever risks he believes the Pill presents to a child. But that doesn't mean he should feel free to withhold information about such risks from those who trust him.

Dr. Walter Larimore, a highly respected and widely published medical researcher, teaches Family Medicine at the University of South Florida and is a member of Focus on the Family's Physician's Resource Council (PRC). In a November 1997 meeting, the majority of the PRC reached the preliminary conclusion that there is no direct primary evidence the Pill causes abortions, and further scientific study is needed. Dr. Larimore and Dr. William Toffler, professor at the Oregon Health Sciences University, are among the PRC minority that has given close attention to the research and is convinced that what we already know about the Pill suggests it poses significant risks to the lives of unborn children.

However, regardless of a physician's personal beliefs on this matter, **it raises the critical issue of informed consent**. In regard to the physician's responsibility to inform women of the possibility the Pill may cause abortions, Dr. Larimore stated to me in a February 26, 1998 email, "True informed consent requires detailed communication. If the physician fails to provide it this seriously jeopardizes a woman's autonomy. Further, **if this information is consciously withheld, it is a breach of ethics**."[124]

Dr. Susan Crockett and her Christian colleagues argue that any abortifacient effect the Pill might have would be so statistically insignificant that patients need not be instructed or worried.[125] But would most patients, exposed to all the medical and scientific sources cited in this book, really believe the chances of a Pill causing an abortion are "statistically insignificant"? Perhaps some would, but certainly many would not. In that light, the question is, "Should physicians act as gatekeepers who withhold access to information that, due to the patients' deeply held ethical and religious beliefs, might persuade them to not use the Pill?"

Prolifers have long been critical of Planned Parenthood and the abortion industry for their consistent refusal to inform women of the development of their unborn children, or show them ultrasound images of those children, or fully inform them of the risks of abortion. "Abortion providers," who have personal and financial vested interests in the matter, often claim it's not in a woman's best interests to be presented with such information. Prolife physicians, who may have personal and financial vested interests in distributing the Pill, must likewise be careful not to rob women of the right to be fully informed of its potential abortive effects. It seems to me that to not practice informed consent regarding the Pill betrays a disrespect for a woman's intelligence, her moral convictions, and her ability to weigh the evidence and make her choice.

If a physician has evidence that the Pill does not cause abortions, he can present that to his patient as well. (I would like to see it myself.) What is the worst-case scenario either way? If a physician makes a patient aware of evidence indicating the Pill may cause early abortions and later research indicates that evidence wasn't valid, what will have been lost? An informed decision has been made on all the available data. But if the physician fails to disclose to her the evidence and it turns out it was true all along, then he has withheld from his patient information that might have kept children from dying and kept his patient's conscience from being violated by a choice made in ignorance.

The Christian Medical and Dental Association has taken a neutral position in the debate about the Pill's abortifacient properties. It concludes by saying "because the possibility of abortive effects cannot be ruled out, prescribers of hormonal birth control should consider informing patients of this potential factor.[126]

The full statement by the CMDA can be found at our website www.epm.org/CMDAstate.html.

The "it's better not to say anything" philosophy puts too much emphasis on us and not enough on the two greatest commandments, loving God and loving our neighbor (Matthew 22:36-40). If we really love God we will want to know the truth so we can act in light of it. If we really love our neighbor, we will want *him* to know the truth so he can do the same. And if we really love our most vulnerable neighbors, the unborn children, we will want to protect and preserve them instead of imperil them through our silence.

Jesus is the truth. Those who serve him are compelled to speak the truth, listen to the truth, and follow the truth in every arena of life, no matter how difficult or inconvenient.

"We've prayed about it and we feel right about using the Pill."

I realize people may sincerely pray and decide it's okay for them to use the Pill. Obviously, everyone must make his own choice. I am not forcing my conclusions on anyone. I am stating my beliefs. One of those beliefs is that the peace or lack of peace one feels after praying can be highly subjective, unless it is specifically rooted in objective truths. There are many people who feel good about doing wrong things and others who feel bad about doing right things. I have seen people make unwise and even catastrophic decisions who told me they prayed and felt good about it.

Often the reason we "feel peace" may be because we are doing what is most comfortable, convenient, natural or widely accepted. None of these is a good reason to believe we are doing right. We need to search the Scriptures to see what is true, and subject ourselves to the authority and guidance of the revealed will of God (Acts 17:11). Then when we call upon God's indwelling Spirit to teach and direct us, he can guide us in light of what he has objectively said to us, not merely what we subjectively feel.

I've heard many people respond to this issue by saying "I just don't feel it's a problem." When I ask for any evidence they know of that refutes that presented in this booklet, they never have any to offer. They say, "I just feel that…" as if having a feeling were somehow a good reason to believe something. "I feel" statements are sincere but subjective; they are not always based on reality. "I think this for these reasons, because of this evidence…" still leaves room for disagreement, but it is far more objective.

One pharmacist who dispenses the Pill stated, "I know it causes abortions, but I pray over each prescription that it won't cause an abortion in the people I'm giving it to." This man should be commended for his sensitive spirit and prayerful attitude. On the other hand, I believe it is unreasonable to dispense a product known to cause abortions and then expect God to answer prayer that it will not work in that way.

If I read studies showing that my family's favorite fruit juice sometimes resulted in fatalities, would I respond by praying they would not die every time I poured them a glass? Or would I just get rid of the fruit juice and never use it again? If I prayed about it and told you I "had a peace" that it was all right to keep serving them this fruit juice despite its proven ability to take human life, if you were my friend, what would you say to me?

"This issue will sidetrack us from fighting surgical abortions."

One prolife physician read a few of the citations in this book and wrote me this: "I think prolifers should stay away from these theoretical arguments and stick with fighting what we know to be wrong: elective induced abortions. We defeat ourselves if we get carried away on tangents arguing about BCPs."

When I examine this evidence, I do not believe it is theoretical. I believe it is real. We don't know how many children are dying from the use of oral contraceptives. It seems apparent that some, likely many, are. Even if you think the evidence isn't conclusive, you must acknowledge that the Pill *may* be killing children. Isn't that at least worth informing people?

As to sticking with fighting "what we know to be wrong," the question is whether we know it is wrong to kill not just the older preborn children but the youngest ones. Or whether we know it is as wrong to kill children with chemicals as with surgical instruments. The answer to both these questions, I believe, is yes. Both result in the deaths of children created in God's image.

The underlying belief seems to be that surgical abortions are "real" and chemical abortions are not. This is true only if older children are more real or valuable than younger ones. This is a fallacy that, of all people, prolife Christians should never buy into. A child is a child, no matter what his age or size.

If human life didn't begin until implantation or thereafter, then concern about the Pill would indeed be sidetracking us from real abortions. But the truth is this—the difference between killing a seven-day-old "zygote" and a seven-week-old "fetus" is exactly the same as between killing a child seven days after birth and killing a child seven weeks after birth. There simply is no difference. Six-day-old children are just as real as six-year-old children, and chemical abortions are just as real as surgical abortions, just as deserving of our concern and action. "Anyone, then, who knows the good he ought to do and doesn't do it, sins" (James 4:17).

Will we as prolifers "defeat ourselves" by speaking up for children killed by chemicals as we do for children killed by surgeries? Or will we just become more consistent and less hypocritical in our advocacy for the unborn?

Is pointing out the abortifacient nature of birth control pills a "tangent" getting us off track, or is it getting us *on* track by obeying God's command to speak up for those who cannot speak for themselves? (Proverbs 31:8-9)

Earlier I cited the paper signed by twenty prolife physicians, affirming that the Pill does not cause abortions. In its conclusion it makes this point:

> How happy the abortionists must be to find us training our guns on a presumption, causing division/confusion among pro-life forces, and taking some of the heat off the abortion industry. Ought we not rather be spending our energies to eliminate the convenient destruction of the innocent unborn?

139

First, our job is to find the truth, even if it causes division or confusion. We should not content ourselves with unity and "certainty" based on ignorance of the truth. (I would also hope that we are mature enough to not be divided simply because we must deal with evidence that is unpleasant.)

Second, we are not taking heat off the abortion industry. I am as much opposed to surgical abortions now as I've been the last seventeen years. In fact, if the Pill sometimes causes abortions, what we are doing is putting heat on another aspect of the abortion industry, the one involved in chemical abortions. Unless we believe it is better to kill a child with chemicals than with surgical instruments, we should oppose all abortions, not just some of them. This is especially true when we consider the future of the abortion industry lies more and more in chemical abortions and increasingly less in surgical ones. Desiring to protect the smallest preborn children from chemical abortions in no way takes away from the importance of protecting bigger preborns from surgical abortion. It is not either/or; it is both/and.

Finally, the statement of some prolife physicians appears to limit "convenience" abortions to surgical ones. It seems not to acknowledge that chemical abortions are every bit as destructive to children, and every bit as displeasing to God. Ironically, by choosing to take hormonal contraceptives when the evidence indicates they put innocent children's lives at risk, don't we unnecessarily run the risk of committing the very "convenience" abortions the statement condemns?

"Prolifers will lose credibility by opposing the Pill."

I recently received a call from a prolife leader who said a physician friend of hers had heard about this book. He told her, "We will all lose credibility if people hear mainstream prolifers opposing the Pill."

What should really make us lose credibility is if we ignore the truth and go right on using the Pill even if it causes abortions. Opposition to abortion demands consistency. We oppose chemical abortions not because we're extremists, but because they do what surgical abortions do: kill children. In many eyes, our opposition to surgical abortions has already lost us credibility. I'm not sure how much credibility we have left to lose in the arena of chemical abortions. But in any case we must never sacrifice truth on the altar of credibility.

The fact that this concern even exists shows how uncritically we as a culture and a Christian community have embraced the Pill. The impression I often get from people's anger and resentment about this issue is, "How *dare* you speak against the Pill?" I'm not talking about the response of nonchristians, but Christians. Is the Pill so sacred that we can't even raise questions concerning it? Is it so much a part of us that we cannot even present scientific evidence and express biblical and ethical concerns without "losing credibility"? If so, then the Pill has taken on the role of a cultural idol, demanding worship and rejecting scrutiny (1 John 5:21).

Even if opposing the abortions caused by the Pill makes us lose credibility with some people, it doesn't change the moral rightness of the position. Integrity before God is more important than credibility before men. We need to carefully and lovingly speak the truth, not bury, ignore or deny it.

The Pill's hold on the Christian community has often surfaced when I've tried to lovingly present the concerns of this book. One person, who described herself as a committed Christian and prolifer, was very upset by this book, and wrote, "We worship God, not fertilized eggs."

Who worships fertilized eggs? Does the writer think those who question the use of the Pill out of concern for newly conceived children are thereby "worshipping fertilized eggs"? As I've said, the term "fertilized eggs" is dehumanizing, and obscures the humanity of the newly conceived child. Saying we don't worship "fertilized eggs" instead of we don't worship "children" may reflect a bias that sees the just-created child as inhuman or less human than older, larger children.

In any case, it is a troubling conclusion that speaking up for the rights of children constitutes "worshipping" them. I believe the basis of our concern for preborn children does not contradict the worship of God, but flows from it. Worship and obedience go hand in hand (Daniel 7:27). If we worship God, and he tells us to feed the hungry, we do it (Matthew 25:31-46). This does not mean we worship the hungry. If someone advocates caring for widows and orphans, I don't say to him, "We worship God, not widows and orphans."

This comment reminds me of the former Surgeon General's statement that prolifers "need to get over their love affair with the fetus." In fact, our love affair is with God. That's why we want to honor and obey him by loving and caring for the smallest children created in his image.

"This puts medical professionals in a very difficult position."

This is something that deeply troubles me. I don't want any of my countless physician friends, brothers and sisters to be made uncomfortable or put on the defensive. Unfortunately, this is one of those issues that will inevitably put them on the spot, especially Ob/GYNs and family practitioners. Other than talking with them, sympathizing with them, and praying for them, I'm not sure what else to do. When discussing this issue it is always relevant to remember that informed consent is a widely accepted ethical mandate of modern medicine.[127] If nonbelievers recognize this, we as believers should take it even more seriously.

I do know that some medical professionals have taken a stand on this issue, and God has been honored by it. One of the physicians who evaluated this book before publication told me she shared the information with a patient, who listened and appreciated hearing the facts. An Ob/Gyn told me that years ago, after coming to realize the Pill causes abortions, he decided he could no longer prescribe it. He informed his patients why. At first, he lost a significant number of patients and income. Ultimately his practice started thriving again, since many prolife people respected his stand and believed they could trust him on matters of principles and ethics. Therefore they sought him out as their physician. Of course, even if he had never regained the lost patients and income, the important thing is he made a decision that honored God.

David Biebel, writing in *Today's Christian Doctor*, relates the story of Ruth Bolton, former head of the family practice residency program at the University of Minnesota Medical School. Dr. Bolton refused to prescribe the Pill and would not train her students in abortion procedures. She observed a growing philosophy in training that placed blame on the medical practitioner if an unexpected pregnancy occurred. Leaving was a difficult decision, but after resigning in 1996, Dr. Bolton started a Christian practice that, as early as 1998, evolved into the fully staffed and thriving Soteria Family Health Center.[128]

Similarly, there are pharmacists who are committed not to distribute the Pill because of their prolife convictions. This can create difficulty and controversy, but sometimes taking a stand for what is right inevitably does that, and people are ultimately informed, challenged and benefited.

California pharmacist John Boling refused to dispense OCs as a "morning after pill," on March 29, 1997. Time, the Associated Press, ABC, CBS, and CNN picked up the story. Boling was reprimanded by his employer, Long's Drug Stores, when he refused to refer the client to another pharmacy for abortifacient pills. Not only Pharmacists for Life but the California Pharmacists Association supported Boling's right of conscience not to dispense chemicals which violate his religious, moral or ethical standards.

Mike Katsonis is a pharmacist for K-Mart in Woods Cross, Utah. He had resigned from the campus dispensary at the University of Florida at Gainesville in 1991 when he refused to fill prescriptions for the "morning after pill." Katsonis has invoked the

Pharmacist's conscience clause and refuses to fill abortifacient prescriptions at K-Mart.

K-Mart's spokesman Dan Jarvis has responded to this refusal by stating "K-Mart will distribute these pills when a doctor prescribes them. We will not tolerate a pharmacist who, on his own because of his own beliefs, will not distribute these medications."[129]

K-Mart fired Indiana pharmacist Karen Brauer for refusing to dispense MicroNor, a progestin-only pill that causes abortions.[130] (Information on the Pharmacist's Conscience Clause is available at Pharmacists for Life's website at www. pfli.org.)

I realize there are some professional sacrifices that might be made by those who act on the belief that the Pill causes abortions. But I am convinced God can be trusted to guide and provide for those willing to make such sacrifices. I also believe the rest of us should be the first to applaud them, stand beside them and support them in every way we can.

Conclusion

In the process of my research I've discovered something I believe all Christians should take very seriously. It is increasingly common in medical literature to find the God-given capacity to bear children viewed not as a blessing to be celebrated but an affliction to be overcome. The FDA, pharmaceuticals and many physicians seem zealously committed to prevent pregnancy as one might labor to prevent obesity or cancer. Women are continuously warned about the "risk" of getting pregnant and are instructed to have back-up birth control in the event an "accident" happens. This is the language of injury, disease and misfortune. The implication is that pregnancy—and the baby who pregnancy is about—is like smallpox or tuberculosis, a disease to be eliminated. The message is not so subtle—children are inconveniences, financial drains and sources of unhappiness. (Except when we really want them, in which case they are adorable and we should spoil them with every material possession known to man.) Rather than be viewed as a blessing—which they are in Scripture and in much of human history—they are often feared and avoided at nearly all costs. The fact that this anti-biblical philosophy permeates so much discussion regarding the Pill should alert us to the fact that we should not consider such sources neutral or objective. They are fully capable of influencing even sincere Christians with anti-children and anti-biblical propaganda.

Many illustrations exist, but one more should suffice. *Contraceptive Technology* is a standard textbook used in medical schools across the country to train medical students in prescribing birth control. Many would assume it to be an objective source of medical information. But the 16th revised edition of this textbook was specifically dedicated to the following: abortion industry organizations, Planned Parenthood Federation and the Feminist Women's Health Centers, as well as the "new [Clinton] leadership in Washington [DC]."[131]

The Problem:
A Spiritual Stronghold?

It is a tragic irony that we who are Christians try to persuade people not to have a single surgical abortion, while as a result of our choice to take the Pill we may be having two, three, a half dozen or more chemical abortions ourselves.

My intention is not to finger-point. I take no glee whatsoever in writing this. Assembling and presenting these materials has not been enjoyable for me. I do not wish to put my brothers and sisters on the defensive. Nor do I assume the worst of them, that they will all ignore this evidence and be callous to the lives of unborn children.

If we'd had the information then that we do now, I am convinced Nanci and I would have stopped using the Pill. In the face of the evidence, I think many others will make the same decision. Of course, I am not naive—I realize that many otherwise prolife people will continue to take the Pill and many Christian physicians will continue to prescribe and recommend it. I do hope that over time this will change, as we become more informed and our consciences become sensitized.

I have spoken with many Christian physicians, brothers I deeply respect, asking them their opinions on this research. Some have said "we need further studies." One said, "I've never heard of any of this before." Another said, "I didn't know about this, but now that I do I can no longer recommend the Pill to my patients." Still another said, "I've heard rumors about this, but no one has ever pointed me to any hard evidence."

I concur that further study is needed and I would be *delighted* if that study contradicted the existing evidence and somehow demonstrated that the Pill is incapable of causing abortions. I would like nothing more than to say, "Though it appeared for a time that the Pill likely causes abortions, new findings refute that notion and assure us it does not." I would gladly retract this book and announce through every means available, "Great news, spread the word—children have not been dying as a result of the Pill; they are not at risk!"

Unless and until such study surfaces, however, the evidence I've presented here, though indirect, is cumulatively very substantial. Some will say "Indirect evidence isn't good enough." My response is, "Show me the evidence, direct *or* indirect, that the Pill never causes abortions." (Don't show me evidence that it *sometimes* doesn't cause abortions, since that isn't the question.)

Can we live with ourselves if we disregard this evidence and say "I won't speak out against the Pill until I have incontrovertible proof it causes abortions and lots of them"? If there is doubt, shouldn't we give the benefit of the doubt to children?

"Does the birth control pill cause abortions?" I do not want to believe it, but I do believe the answer is "yes." But even if I wasn't sure I would have to say the evidence compels me to oppose the Pill unless definitive evidence is produced to indicate it does not cause abortions.

"Then, does that mean we should believe something when there's no direct proof of it?" No matter which position we take, we *already* believe something there's no direct proof of. Is there direct proof the Pill causes abortions? No. Is there direct proof the Pill doesn't cause abortions? No. Is there indirect evidence the Pill causes abortions? Yes, a lot of it. Is there indirect evidence it doesn't cause abortions? I'm not certain there is, but if there is I believe it is less than persuasive.

In the face of the evidence, our position on the Pill offers a great test of our true convictions. Do we really believe God creates every human life at the point of conception, six days before implantation begins? And will we exercise this conviction even at the cost of our personal convenience?

Perhaps what we thought was a conviction will be proven to be no more than a preference. Maybe the truth is, if we can avoid abortion without inconvenience to ourselves we will do so, but if it requires extra effort on our part, we will go ahead and risk the lives of our children. (In fact, they are really not "our" children to risk—they are created by God and owned by God, and entrusted to us by him to protect and nurture.)

There are some very disturbing questions we need to ask.

Can God, who creates each human life at the point of conception, fully bless the efforts of prolife organizations, volunteers and staff members, of sidewalk counselors and pastors and doctors—any of us—when we turn right around and use, prescribe or recommend a product that sometimes takes the life of an unborn child?

Are we consistently prolife or only selectively prolife? Do we oppose later abortions while not really caring about the earliest ones? Is the only difference between us and those we call "proabortion" that they are willing to embrace the killing of bigger and older children while we are willing to embrace the killing only of smaller and younger children? Are we moral relativists and gradualists different only in degree but not in kind with those we call abortionists?

Because we have grown so accustomed to the Pill, will we turn our heads away from the risks it poses to our children? Do we dare to play God by infringing upon his sole and sacred prerogatives over human life?

We often encounter proabortion people who deny the basic medical and moral realities of the issue, and sometimes we shake our heads in wonder at the extent of their denial of the obvious, that abortion kills children and that it is therefore morally repugnant. Even many who are otherwise prolife live in denial when they say, "I oppose abortion, except in cases of rape, incest and deformity." (Of course, an unborn child is a child; regardless of how he was conceived and what his handicaps are, it is wrong to kill a child.)

When it comes to something so deeply entrenched in our society and in the Christian community as the Pill, even the most prolife people are fully capable of denial. Looking back, I believe I was in denial on this issue from the time I first heard about it in 1991. Why didn't I dig deeper? Why didn't I research it more carefully?

I can come up with many other reasons to explain it away, but perhaps the bottom line is, **I just didn't want it to be true**. But there are many things I don't want to be true that still are. I don't want to believe there is an eternal hell; or that as a Christian I will be held accountable for my works at the judgment seat of Christ; or that millions of children go to bed hungry each night; or that abortion kills children; or that the Pill causes abortions. I don't want to believe any of these things, but I believe each of them nonetheless because the evidence demonstrates them to be true.

Is there a supernatural reason for our ignorance and denial on this issue? As much as I believe in the spiritual realm and the spiritual battle, I am not quick to attribute every misunderstanding or problem in the church to demonic influence. However, consider what Jesus said: "the devil…was a murderer from the beginning, not holding to the truth, for there is no truth in him. When he lies, he speaks his native language, for he is a liar and the father of lies" (John 8:44).

When Satan carries out murder in an outwardly "civil" society, inevitably he must bury the murder in a huge grave of lies so that no one sees the corpses. (As Stalin put it, "One death is a tragedy; a million deaths is a statistic.") When Satan convinces the church of these lies he has achieved his greatest victory—it's hard to imagine a more horrid irony or a more crippling blow to the church than that we, followers of Christ, would make choices that result in the deaths of our own children.

The biggest threat to Satan's success in killing the innocent is that people become aware of the truth, then act on it. When I consider my own ignorance and lack of motivation to pursue and act on the truth that the Pill kills children, I am forced to conclude this may well be a spiritual stronghold that the evil one has on the church. Until we come to grips with, repent of and abstain from the chemical abortions we ourselves are having, I wonder how effective we will be as Christ's representatives in general, and in particular in our efforts to prevent abortions. (Looking back, we haven't been very successful in our efforts to curtail surgical abortions–perhaps this is one of the reasons.)

The Trend: Chemical versus Surgical Abortions

Many surgical abortions happen in Christian churches, far more than most people realize. According to the latest Guttmacher Institute study, nearly one out of five women getting surgical abortions claims to be a born again Christian. At least in thousands of churches across the country there is *some* voice against surgical abortions. But chemical abortions are going almost completely unchallenged, even in the most prolife churches and organizations.

Ironically, it is chemical abortions that are the clear direction of abortion in America and around the world.

Trends indicate that in years to come there will be fewer surgical abortions, mostly because of the popularity and "ease" of chemical abortions. If the church herself is committing chemical abortions as a way of life, then we are woefully unprepared to fight the abortion battle at any level, and certainly not this one.

Many prolife groups that have exclusively targeted surgical abortions will celebrate as great victories the fact that in years to come more and more abortion clinics will shut down and there will be fewer doctors doing surgical abortions. But it will only be a true victory if it means less children are being killed.

It appears this is *not* what it will mean. Every indication is that more physicians who did not do surgical abortions will dispense chemical abortifacients to their patients. A 1995 Kaiser survey showed that many doctors who would not perform surgical abortions would prescribe the abortion pill, RU-486.[132]

Celebrating the demise of surgical abortion clinics while chemical abortions take their place would be like celebrating the fact that less Jews were being killed in the gas ovens because most were now being killed by lethal injections. Our point should not be merely to oppose a certain method of killing babies, but to oppose the killing of babies by any and all methods.

Ironically, the move to chemical abortifacients brings us full circle, since it is actually a return to the ancient way of doing abortions. In times when surgical abortions were very rare, abortionists, who were often apothecaries or unethical doctors with knowledge of what chemicals induced miscarriages, provided certain herbs, chemicals and poisons to women.

That's why the ancient Hippocratic Oath taken by physicians stated, "I will give no deadly medicine to anyone if asked, nor suggest such counsel, and in like manner, I will not give to a woman a pessary to produce an abortion." A pessary was an oval stone inserted in the vagina, which could be used to cause an abortion.

As the IUD is parallel to the "pessary" (a physical device) prohibited by the Oath, so the Pill and other chemical abortifacients are parallel to the "deadly medicine" ethical physicians would not prescribe.

Chemical Abortions: History and Scripture

It was in the face of such chemical and device-caused abortions that Christian leaders in the first few centuries consistently denounced all abortions. For instance, in about AD 200, Minucius Felix wrote in *Octavius*, "There are women who swallow drugs to stifle in their own womb the beginnings of a man to be—committing infanticide before they even give birth to the infant." In the fourth century Basil the Great wrote, "Those who give abortifacients for the destruction of a child conceived in the womb are murderers themselves, along with those receiving the poisons." **(See *Appendix C*, Abortion: Perspectives of the Early Church Leaders.)**

In fact, a strong case can be made for understanding the Greek word translated "sorcery" in Galatians 5:20 as a reference to administering drugs to commit abortions. This word is "*pharmakeia*," from which we get our word "pharmaceuticals," or drugs. The administering of drugs and potions was common in sorcery, and hence the word sometimes took on that secondary connotation. But it is also used in the Greek literature of the day with its original primary meaning of drugs, chemicals or medications. The most prevalent social example of the evil use of chemicals was administering them to induce abortions. Early in the second century, the physician Soranos of Ephesus, in his book *Gynecology*, used *pharmakeia* referring specifically to drugs that cause abortions.

Galatians 5:20 lists *pharmakeia,* translated "witchcraft" in the NIV, as one of the "acts of the sinful nature." It precedes It with listing sexual immorality, impurity, debauchery and idolatry. All of these relate to the sexually immoral practices that led to many unwanted children and therefore many abortions, giving further credence to the idea that *pharmakeia* may in fact refer to, or at least include, using chemicals to kill unborn children.

The same word is used three times in Revelation. In Revelation 9:21 it says: "Nor did they repent of their murders, their *pharmakeus*, their sexual immorality or their thefts." In 21:8 it states: "But the cowardly, the unbelieving, the vile, the murderers, the sexually immoral, the *pharmakeus*, the idolaters and all liars— their place will be in the fiery lake of burning sulfur." In Revelation 22:15 it says, "Outside are the dogs, the *pharmakeus*, the sexually immoral, the murderers, the idolaters and everyone who loves and practices falsehood."

Even if these Scriptural passages do not refer to chemical abortions—we cannot be certain one way or the other—everything else we know of Scripture and church history tells us we should oppose all forms of abortion with vigor and consistency.

As the devil loved the sacrifice of children in the ancient heathen cultures, so he loves the sacrifice of children in our modern culture. Whether children are sacrificed to a heathen god called Molech or to the god of our own convenience, he does not care. (See *Appendix F:* **The Shedding of Innocent Blood.**) Whether these children are born or unborn does not matter to the Murderer from the beginning, for each of them is equally created in the image of God, and by killing them he comes as close as he can to striking out at God himself. In killing those created in his image, Satan kills God in effigy.

The evil one's vested interests in our blindness on this issue cannot be overstated. The forces of darkness desperately do not want us to see these newly conceived children as their Creator sees them. If we are to come over to God's way of thinking about them, it will only be through searching the Scriptures, praying, examining the evidence and openly and boldly addressing this issue in our churches and Christian organizations.

Time to Search our Hearts and Ways?

Christian couples who are using the Pill, isn't it time to sit down and have a heart-to-heart talk? As a matter of conscience and conviction, do you believe you can or should continue with the Pill? Is it time to consider other alternatives? Time to search the Scriptures together, pray together, look at the facts presented here, and ask God's guidance for your family? The choice is yours to make—make it prayerfully, with a Christ-centered commitment to putting principle above convenience.

Pastors, counselors, physicians, nurses, pharmacists and others: what will you do with this information? Our churches, our patients, our counselees, and our families look to us for leadership. Let's take our God-given role seriously and provide that leadership. At the very least we must present people with both the scientific facts and the biblical principles, so they can be informed enough to make wise and godly decisions. We dare not be silent in the face of the lives of children created in the image of God. "Speak up for those who cannot speak up for themselves; defend the rights of the poor and needy" (Proverbs 31:8-9). (See *Appendix H:* **Defending the Weak and Helpless)**

I have deep empathy for my Christian brothers and sisters who are Ob/GYNs and family practitioners. For many years, most of them have recommended and prescribed the Pill to their patients, unaware of its abortifacient aspects. I know this information places them in a terribly difficult position. I realize it would be extremely difficult for them to present the evidence to their patients and explain why they can no longer do so. I also know that God will bless those who make such sacrifices for what is right and true, not only in this arena but also in others.

I encourage pastors to counsel and stand beside medical professionals who face misunderstanding and resistance from patients and public. We should admire, commend and encourage their principled actions.

I also encourage pastors to speak out directly on this issue in their churches. I was a pastor for fourteen years, and I realize this will not be easy. Some people will be angry and defensive—I know, I've gotten some of their letters. But others will be thankful and appreciative, and will seek God's face and genuinely deal with this issue. We owe our people the truth, and the opportunity to respond to it. In any case, **the issue is not whether people will applaud our decision to address this subject. The issue is whether the Audience of One desires us to do so. If he does, all other opinions are irrelevant**.

If you are not satisfied with the evidence presented here, will you commit yourself to find out the truth? Go to the Scriptures first, then go to the medical journals and textbooks. Call the Pill manufacturers. Of course, you must be prepared for the fact that they have been trained to deal with questions in a way to minimize or eliminate concerns about abortion. Even then, if you persist in your questions, most of them will acknowledge that their literature is correct—the Pill *does* sometimes prevent implantation of a newly conceived human being. They will still say that even when the blastocyst, which you recognize to be a person created in God's image, is prevented from implanting "there is no pregnancy" and "the Pill is not an abortifacient." You will know better.

If after investigating the issue, you still are not convinced, ask yourself "If *this* evidence doesn't convince me, is there any evidence that would?" Is it possible—I ask this cautiously and not critically—that your own vested interests in this issue are blinding you to the truth? In other words, if you didn't have something to lose by believing and acting upon this evidence, would you still reject it? Is the real problem lack of evidence or is it that you are determined not to change your beliefs and practice despite the evidence?

It's always better to live in the light than the darkness, even if for the moment the darkness may be comforting to the eye. Ultimately, facing the truth will set us free. Denying it will put us in bondage. The evidence concerning the Pill may disturb us—it certainly disturbs me—but if we respond prayerfully to what we know, we can make informed choices to affirm Christ's Lordship over our families our churches and us. God will surely bless us for that.

Let God's Word be the final one: "This day I call heaven and earth as witnesses against you that I have set before you life and death, blessings and curses. Now **choose life, so that you and your children may live**" (Deuteronomy 30:19).

Note from the author:

Feel free to photocopy this book and give it to your friends, family, church or anyone else. You have my full permission to do so.

You may find it more convenient and less expensive to order printed copies of this book from Eternal Perspective Ministries. Contact us at 503-668-5200, info@epm.org, or 39085 Pioneer Blvd., Suite 206, Sandy, OR 97055 (Fax: 503-668-5252.)

The book's cost is $3.00 for a single copy, $2.50 each for 2-9 copies, $2.25 each for 10-99, $2.00 each for 100-499, and $1.75 each for 500 or more. (Add 10% shipping, 7% shipping for orders of 100 copies or more.)

If anyone has information—particularly primary sources—refuting or supporting any claims of this book, please send it to me at the above address or to info@epm.org. I will revise this book as needed with each new printing. I will also publish any relevant responses, including arguments and evidence from those who disagree, at our EPM website at www.epm.org.

We especially invite physicians, pharmacists or other medical personnel to send comments, criticisms or endorsements. I also want to invite you to my blog at www.randyalcorn.blogspot.com. Thank you.

Appendices

Appendix A: When Does Each Human Life Begin? The Answer of Scripture

"The **babies** [Jacob and Esau] jostled each other within her [Rebekah]." (Genesis 25:22)

"If men fight and hurt a woman with child, so that she gives birth prematurely…" (Exodus 21:22)

"As you do not know…how the bones grow in the womb of her who is with child…" (Ecclesiastes 11:5)

Note: in each of the above references God calls that which a pregnant woman carries a "child."

"In the womb **he** [Jacob] grasped his brother's heel; as a man **he** struggled with God." (Hosea 12:3)

"**Your hands shaped me and made me**. Will you now turn and destroy me? Remember that **you molded me like clay**. Will you now turn me to dust again? Did you not pour me out like milk and curdle me like cheese, **clothe me with skin and flesh and knit me together with bones and sinews**? You gave me life and showed me kindness, and **in your providence watched over my spirit**." (Job 10:8-12)

"Did not he who made me in the womb make them? **Did not the same one form us both within our mothers?**" (Job 31:15)

"For you created my inmost being; **you knit me together in my mother's womb**. I praise you because I am fearfully and wonderfully made…My frame was not hidden from you when I was made in the secret place. When I was woven together in the depths of the earth, **your eyes saw my unformed body**. All the days ordained for me were written in your book before one of them came to be." (Psalm 139:13-16)

"Surely I was sinful at birth; **sinful from the time my mother conceived me**." (Psalm 51:5)

Note: Only a person can have a sin nature. David's statement clearly shows he was a person at the point of conception.

"**Before I formed you in the womb I knew you**, before you were born I set you apart; I appointed you as a prophet to the nations." (Jeremiah 1:5)

"His mother Mary… as found to **be with child** through the Holy Spirit…[the angel said] '**what is conceived in her is from the Holy Spirit**.'" (Matthew 1:18-20)

"But the angel said to Mary 'you will be **with child** and give birth to a son, and you are to give him the name Jesus…The Holy Spirit **will** come upon you, and the power of the Most High **will** overshadow you. So the holy one to be born will be called the Son of God.'" (Luke 1:30-31, 35)

Summary of Luke 1:39-44: *After the angel left, Mary "hurried" (v. 39) to get to Elizabeth. Unborn John the Baptist (in his 6th month after conception) responded to the presence of unborn Jesus inside Mary. Allowing for travel time, Jesus was no more than eight to ten*

days beyond conception when they arrived.
Implantation doesn't begin until six days after
*conception and isn't complete until twelve—**most***
likely Jesus was not yet fully implanted in his
mother's womb when unborn John responded to
his presence.

"The Word became flesh and made his dwelling
among us. We have seen his glory, the glory of the
One and Only, who came from the Father, full of
grace and truth." (John 1:14)

When did the Word (Christ) become flesh? When did
he leave heaven and come to earth? Was there
generic soul-less flesh conceived in Mary waiting for
Christ to inhabit it later in the pregnancy? No—it is
basic Christian doctrine that Christ became flesh at
the moment the Holy Spirit overshadowed Mary, at
the moment of fertilization. He became human at the
exact point all others become human, the point of
conception. The "blastocyst" is an eternal human soul,
literally "the least of these [vulnerable people],"
Christ's brethren (Matthew 25:40).

Appendix B: When Does Each Human Life Begin? The Answer of Science

Dr. Alfred M. Bongioanni, professor of obstetrics, University of Pennsylvania:

> "I have learned from my earliest medical education that **human life begins at the time of conception**. I submit that human life is present throughout this entire sequence from conception to adulthood and any interruption at any point throughout this time constitutes a termination of human life."

Dr. Jerome LeJeune, genetics professor at the University of Descartes in Paris (discoverer of the Down Syndrome chromosome):

> "After fertilization has taken place a new human being has come into being…This is no longer a matter of taste or opinion. **Each individual has a very neat beginning, at conception.**"

Professor Micheline Matthews-Roth, Harvard University Medical School:

> "It is scientifically correct to say that **an individual human life begins at conception.**"

Professor Hymie Gordon, Mayo Clinic:

> "By all the criteria of modern molecular biology, **life is present from the moment of conception.**"

Dr. Watson A. Bowes, University of Colorado Medical School:

> "The beginning of a single human life is from a biological point of view a simple and straightforward matter—**the beginning is conception**."

Dr. Landrum Shettles, pioneer in sperm biology, fertility and sterility, discoverer of male- and female-producing sperm:

> "I oppose abortion. I do so, first, because I accept what is biologically manifest—that **human life commences at the time of conception**—and, second, because I believe it is wrong to take innocent human life under any circumstances."

Appendix C: Abortion: Perspectives of the Early Church Leaders

"Do not murder a child by abortion or kill a new-born infant." (*The Didache* 2.2)
"The Way of Death is filled with people who are...murderers of children and abortionists of God's creatures." (*The Didache* 5:1-2)

Note: *The Didache* was a second century (AD 120) catechism for young Christian converts. The inclusion of these statements shows that instruction not to commit abortion was a basic and essential Christian teaching, not a fringe or secondary issue.

"You shall love your neighbor more than your own life. You shall not slay a child by abortion. You shall not kill that which has already been generated." (*Epistle of Barnabas* 19.5; 125 AD)

"We say that women who induce abortions are murderers, and will have to give account of it to God. For the same person would not regard the child in the womb as a living being and therefore an object of God's care and then kill it...But we are altogether consistent in our conduct. We obey reason and do not override it." (Athenagoras, *Legatio 35*, AD 165)

"The fetus in the womb is a living being and therefore the object of God's care." (Athenagoras, *A Plea for the Christians*, 35.6; AD 177)

"It does not matter whether you take away a life that is born, or destroy one that is coming to the birth. In both instances, the destruction is murder." (Tertullian, *Apology*, 9.4-6; second century)

"Our whole life can go on in observation of the laws of nature, if we gain dominion over our desires from the beginning and if we do not kill, by various means of a perverse art, the human offspring, born according to the designs of divine providence; for these women who, in order to hide their immorality, use abortive drugs which expel the child completely dead, abort at the same time their own human feelings." (Clement of Alexandria, *Paedagogus* 2, AD 175)

"Reputed believers began to resort to drugs for producing sterility and to gird themselves round, so as to expel what was conceived on account of their not wanting to have a child either by a slave of by any paltry fellow, for the sake of their family and excessive wealth. Behold, into how great impiety that lawless one has proceeded by inculcating adultery and murder at the same time." (Hippolytus, *Refutation of all Heresies* 9:7, AD 200)

"The wealthy, in order that their inheritance may not be divided among several, deny in the very womb their own progeny. By use of parricidal mixtures they snuff out the fruit of their wombs in the genital organs themselves. In this way life is taken away before it is born…Who except man himself has taught us ways of repudiating children?" (Ambrose of Milan, *Hexameron*, c. AD 350)

"Those who give abortifacients for the destruction of a child conceived in the womb are murderers themselves, along with those receiving the poisons." (Basil the Great, *Canons*, 188.2; fourth century)

"Thou shalt not slay thy child by causing abortion, nor kill that which is begotten. For everything that is shaped, and has received a soul from God, if slain, it shall be avenged, as being unjustly destroyed." *(The Apostolic Constitutions* 73; AD 380)

"Why sow where the ground makes it its care to destroy the fruit? Where there are many efforts at abortion? Where there is murder before birth? For you do not even let the harlot remain a mere harlot, but make her a murderer also. You see how drunkenness leads to whoredom, whoredom to adultery, adultery to murder; or rather something even worse than murder. For I have no real name to give it, since it does not destroy the thing born but prevents its being born. Why then do you abuse the gift of God and fight with His laws, and follow after what is a curse as if a blessing, and make the place of procreation a chamber for murder, and arm the woman that was given for childbearing unto slaughter?" (John Chrysostom, *Homily 24 on Romans*, c. AD 375)

Jerome called abortion "the murder of an unborn child" (*Letter to Eustochium*, 22.13; fourth century). Augustine used the same phrase, warning against the terrible crime of "the murder of an unborn child" (*On Marriage*, 1.17.15, fourth century).

"The fetus, though enclosed in the womb of its mother, is already a human being and it is a most monstrous crime to rob it of the life which it has not yet begun to enjoy. If it seems more horrible to kill a man in his own house than in a field, because a man's house is his place of most secure refuge, it ought surely to be deemed more atrocious to destroy a fetus in the womb before it has come to light." (John Calvin, sixteenth century reformer)

Appendix D: God is Creator and Owner of All People (and therefore has sole rights over all)

"So God created man **in his own image**, in the image of God he created him; male and female he created them." (Genesis 1:27)

Know that the Lord Himself is God: **it is He who has made us, and not we ourselves**; we are His people and the sheep of His pasture." (Psalm 100:3, NASV)

"For **every living soul belongs to me**, the father as well as the son." (Ezekiel 18:4)

"Yet, O LORD, you are our Father. We are the clay, you are the potter; **we are all the work of your hand**." (Isaiah 64:8)

"Do you not know that your body is a temple of the Holy Spirit, who is in you, whom you have received from God? **You are not your own**; you were bought at a price. Therefore **honor God with your body**." (1 Corinthians 6:19-20)

Appendix E: God has Exclusive Prerogatives Over Human Life and Death

"See now that I myself am He! There is no god besides me. **I put to death and I bring to life**, I have wounded and I will heal, and no one can deliver out of my hand." (Deuteronomy 32:39)

"The LORD brings death and makes alive; he brings down to the grave and raises up." (1 Samuel 2:6)

"You shall not commit murder." (Exodus 20:13)

Note: Except when he specifically delegates that right to men (e.g. capital punishment, self defense, just war), God alone has the right to take a human life.

"And for your lifeblood I will surely demand an accounting...And from each man, too, **I will demand an accounting for the life of his fellow man.**" (Genesis 9:5)

"If men who are fighting hit a pregnant woman and she gives birth prematurely but there is no serious injury, the offender must be fined whatever the woman's husband demands and the court allows. But if there is serious injury, you are to take life for life, eye for eye, tooth for tooth, hand for hand, foot for foot, burn for burn, wound for wound, bruise for bruise." (Exodus 21:22-25)

"Nothing in all creation is hidden from God's sight. Everything is uncovered and laid bare before the eyes of him to whom we must give account." (Hebrews 4:13)

Appendix F:
The Shedding of Innocent Blood

"Do not give any of your children to be sacrificed to Molech, for you must not profane the name of your God. I am the LORD." (Leviticus 18:21)

"The LORD said...'Any Israelite or any alien living in Israel who gives any of his children to Molech must be put to death. The people of the community are to stone him...**by giving his children to Molech, he has defiled my sanctuary and profaned my holy name**...If the people of the community **close their eyes** when that man gives one of his children to Molech...I will set my face against that man and his family and will cut off from their people both him and all who follow him...'" (Leviticus 20:1-5)

"Do this **so that innocent blood will not be shed in your land**, which the LORD your God is giving you as your inheritance, and **so that you will not be guilty of bloodshed**." (Deuteronomy 19:10)

"The LORD sent Babylonian, Aramean, Moabite and Ammonite raiders against him. He sent them to destroy Judah, in accordance with the word of the LORD proclaimed by his servants the prophets. Surely these things happened to Judah according to the Lord's command, in order to remove them from his presence *because of the sins of Manasseh and all he had done, including the shedding of innocent blood.* For **he filled Jerusalem with innocent blood**, and the LORD was not willing to forgive." (2 Kings 24:2-4)

171

"The LORD said, 'What have you done? Listen! **Your brother's blood cries out to me from the ground.'**" (Genesis 4:10)

"For God will deliver the needy who cry out, the afflicted who have no one to help. He will take pity on the weak and the needy and save the needy from death. He will rescue them from oppression and violence, for **precious is their blood in his sight**." (Psalm 72:12-14)

"There are six things the LORD hates, seven that are detestable to him: haughty eyes, a lying tongue, **hands that shed innocent blood**..." (Proverbs 6:16-19)

"Therefore as surely as I live, declares the Sovereign LORD, I will give you over to bloodshed and it will pursue you. **Since you did not hate bloodshed, bloodshed will pursue you.**" (Ezekiel 35:6)

Appendix G:
How God Sees Children

"See that you do not look down on one of these little ones. For I tell you that their angels in heaven always see the face of my Father in heaven." (Matthew 18:10)

"But Jesus called the children to him and said, "Let the little children come to me, and do not hinder them, for the kingdom of God belongs to such as these." (Luke 18:16)

"Your Father in heaven is not willing that any of these little ones should be lost." (Matthew 18:14)

"Sons are a heritage from the LORD, children a reward from him." (Psalm 127:3-4)

Appendix H:
Defending the Weak and Helpless

"**Defend the cause of the weak and fatherless**;
maintain the rights of the poor and oppressed.
Rescue the weak and needy; deliver them from
the hand of the wicked." (Psalm 82:3-4)

"**Rescue those being led away to death; hold
back those staggering toward slaughter**. If you
say, 'But we knew nothing about this,' does not he
who weighs the heart perceive it? Does not he
who guards your life know it? Will he not repay
each person according to what he has done?"
(Proverbs 24:11-12)

"**Speak up for those who cannot speak for
themselves, for the rights of all who are
destitute**. Speak up and judge fairly; **defend the
rights of the poor and needy**." (Proverbs 31:8-9)

"Anyone, then, who **knows the good he ought to
do and doesn't do it, sins**." (James 4:17)

"House of David, this is what the LORD says:
'Administer justice every morning; **rescue from
the hand of his oppressor the one who has
been robbed, or my wrath will break out and
burn like fire because of the evil you have
done**—burn with no one to quench it.'" (Jeremiah
21:12)

"Then the King will say to those on his right,
'Come...**take your inheritance**, the kingdom
prepared for you since the creation of the world.
For I was hungry and you gave me something

to eat, I was thirsty and you gave me something to drink, I was a stranger and you invited me in, **I needed clothes and you clothed me**, I was sick and you looked after me, I was in prison and you came to visit me…I tell you the truth, **whatever you did for one of the least of these brothers of mine, you did for me.**' Then he will say to those on his left, 'Depart from me…For I was hungry and **you gave me nothing to eat**, I was thirsty and you gave me nothing to drink, I was a stranger and you did not invite me in, I needed clothes and **you did not clothe me**, I was sick and in prison and **you did not look after me**'…'I tell you the truth, **whatever you did *not* do for one of the least of these, you did *not* do for me.**'" (Matthew 25:31-46)

Appendix I: Other Contraceptives"
that Cause Abortions

The IUD, Norplant, Depo-Provera & RU 486

Prolifers have long opposed using the IUD, because it does not prevent conception, but keeps the already-conceived child from implanting in his mother's womb.

A paper by Irving Sivin challenges this understanding.[133] Since other evidence has suggested it is an abortifacient, the jury appears to still be out on the IUD. However, because the stakes are so high, the uncertainty argues against using the IUD.

RU-486, the anti-progestin abortion pill, is a human pesticide causing a mother's womb to become hostile to her own child, resulting in an induced miscarriage.[134]

Depo-Provera is a progestin (medroxyprogesterone) injected every three months. It sometimes suppresses ovulation, but also thins the lining of the uterus, apparently preventing implantation.

Norplant is another progestin (levonorgestrel) enclosed in five or six flexible closed capsules or rods, which are surgically implanted beneath the skin. It often suppresses ovulation, but sometimes ovulation occurs, and when it does an irritation to the uterine wall may often prevent implantation.

The Emergency Contraceptive Pill (ECP) also known as the "Morning-After Pill," can suppress ovulation, but its main function is to keep any fertilized egg from implanting in the uterus.

All of these birth control methods either sometimes or often alter the mother's womb in a way that causes it to reject the human life that God designed it to nourish and sustain.

Christians properly reject these methods because they know that human life begins at conception, six days before implantation begins. Therefore, anything that interferes with implantation kills a person created in the image of God.

These birth control methods are often referred to as "contraceptives," but they are *not* exclusively contraceptives. That is, they do not always prevent conception. Either sometimes or often they result in the death of already-conceived human beings.

The Mini-Pill (Progestin-only)

Progestin-only pills, which have no estrogen, are often called "Mini-pills." Many people confuse Mini-pills with the far more popular combination estrogen-progestin pills, which are the true "Birth Control Pill."

Drug Facts & Comparisons is a standard reference book for physicians. It says this under "Oral Contraceptives":

> Oral contraceptives (OCs) include estrogen-progestin combos and progestin-only products. Progestin-only [pills]…alter the cervical mucus, exert a progestational effect on the endometrium, apparently producing cellular changes that render the endometrium hostile to implantation by a fertilized ovum (egg) and, in some patients, suppress ovulation.[135]

177

Note that progestin-only pills have as a primary effect to make the uterine lining, the endometrium, "**hostile to implantation by a fertilized ovum**." In other words, they cause an abortion of a human being roughly a week after his or her conception.

I have been told that many users of the Mini-pill think their ovulations are being suppressed. In fact, some new mothers have gone on the Mini-pill in order to prevent pregnancy while breast-feeding. However, in his book *Gynecology: Principles & Practices*, R.W. Kistner says, "Certainly the majority of women using the progestin-only pill continue to ovulate."[136]

In his book *Hormonal Contraception: Pills, Injections & Implants*, Dr. Joseph W. Goldzieher, states, "**Endometrial resistance to implantation is an important mechanism of the minipill**."[137]

A 1981 Searle leaflet, packaged with their progestin-only pill, says that product "**makes the womb less receptive to any fertilized egg that reaches it**."[138]

The Physician's Desk Reference describes "Progestogen-Only Oral Contraceptives" by saying they "are known to alter the cervical mucus and exert a progestational effect on the endometrium, **interfering with implantation**."[139]

Clearly the progestin-only pill, by its effects on the endometrium, causes abortions and must be added to the list of abortive birth control methods. Like all the aforementioned products, the changes the Mini-pill creates in the mother's endometrium make the womb hostile to the newly-conceived child, instead of hospitable to him, as God designed the mother's womb to be.

Appendix J: Randy Alcorn's response to Dr. Joel Goodnough's article, "Redux: Is the oral contraceptive pill an abortifacient?" Ethics and Medicine 2001;17:37-51. (Response submitted to the journal August 2001.)

In the spring of 2001, a well-respected Christian journal, *Ethics & Medicine* published an article by a brother in Christ, Dr. Joel Goodnough, an attempt to refute the research that went into preparing an earlier edition of this book as well as some of my own conclusions. Goodnough asserts that there are three central issues to be addressed:

> The central question that Alcorn asks is whether the OCP exclusively acts as a contraceptive or whether it sometimes prevents implantation, and therefore causes abortion...Does the OCP cause early loss of the embryo at all, infrequently, or frequently? And if it does cause abortion, does that make it an abortifacient? If we cannot decide if the OCP causes abortions, what should we do? To answer these questions, we must assess the pill's ability to prevent fertilization and then try to determine the consequences to the embryo when the pill fails to do so. Finally, we have to decide how to live in an imperfect world with risks (p. 37).

The article is lengthy and because of space limitations it cannot be reproduced here. You may wish to contact *Ethics & Medicine* for a complete copy of what he has written. I encourage you to carefully read all that he has to say.

After the article appeared I wrote to *Ethics & Medicine*. What follows is my response to Dr. Goodnough's article:

I read with interest Dr. Goodnough's article on the abortifacient effect of the oral contraceptive pill (OCP). One thing Dr. Goodnough and I share in common is that we both very much hope his theories are correct–and that my view of the evidence is eventually disproved. As one whose wife took oral contraceptives, and who for many years recommended oral contraceptives in premarital counseling—and who doesn't want for a moment to believe children may have been killed by my actions taken out of ignorance—I would certainly like to believe Dr. Goodnough's position. If one day he is proved right, I will rejoice. Unfortunately the evidence I've found, through painstaking research, does not support his conclusions. Futhermore, he made a number of factual errors of which the objective reader and a peer-reviewed journal such as *Ethics and Medicine* would want to be informed.

Some of the weaknesses of Dr. Goodnough's article have been pointed out by Dr. Walter Larimore, in his letter to the editor of *Ethics and Medicine*. These include, but are not limited to, the following: 1) In citing the 3% pregnancy rate for first-year pill-takers, Dr. Goodnough fails to take into account the fact that women who get pregnant while taking the pill and then get abortions are counted statistically as if they've never gotten pregnant at all, making the actual first-year pregnancy rate in pill takers much higher. 2) Dr. Goodnough's "turned on endometrium" theory is completely speculative, and he presents no scientific evidence supporting it. 3) By using a dated version of my book (1998, instead of the 2000 edition, which is three revisions later), and by drawing my quotes from a now long-dated email exchange with Dr. Larimore rather than Dr. Larimore's subsequent article in *Archives of Family Medicine*, Dr. Goodnough significantly misrepresented several of my and Larimore's conclusions.

My major concerns about Dr. Goodnough's article involve its considerable logical and ethical weaknesses, as well as one particularly serious misquotation of my book.

Dr. Goodnough asks, "Is the OCP an abortifacient? Or is it a contraceptive that has the potential for failure, a failure that may result in the death of the embryo?" (It's interesting that he narrows it down to these two choices, an apparent admission that the Pill may indeed result in the death of a child—which, ironically, is the central point that I present in my book.) He cites a medical dictionary's definition of an abortifacient being something deliberately used to cause an abortion. Then he argues that the Pill isn't an abortifacient, since people don't deliberately use it to cause abortions. But this isn't the point. The issue isn't what the OCP should be called, it's what the OCP can do. My book's title is not "Should the Birth Control Pill Be called an Abortifacient?" but "Can the Birth Control Pill Cause Abortions?" The latter question, not the former, is what this is all about.

Dr. Goodnough gives considerable attention to semantics. He insists "a medication that is used to prevent conception is not an abortifacient even if it sometimes causes an abortion." But the young men and women who talk to me about this issue are never concerned about labels and terminology. Their question is simple—can taking the Pill result in the unrecognized death of a pre-born child? Though at times he seems to deny it, at other times Dr. Goodnough appears to admit the answer is yes. Given what he regards as the positives of OCPs, he considers this a risk worth taking. Many couples, however, do not.

One of my main points is that couples have the right to know this information and the medical community has the legal and ethical obligation to inform them. This is why Dr. Larimore and I and others have simply encouraged physicians and health-care systems to provide full information to patients. If the patient is interested, show them the evidence, and let them come to their own conclusions. This is the crux of informed consent. But is it ethical for a physician to withhold evidence that many people—including other well-respected physicians—believe supports the contention of the Food and Drug Administration (FDA) and the OCP companies that the Pill sometimes prevents the implantation of a newly conceived child? Conscientious Christians who put their prolife convictions above their convenience are not unusual, and they are not stupid. They can handle the evidence and reach their own conclusions. They will be held accountable for their choices, just as we will be held accountable for whether or not we present them with the full body of evidence.

As I clearly state in the book, usually the birth control pill does *not* cause abortions. As far as I am aware, no one argues that it usually acts as an abortifacient. The question is whether it *sometimes* causes the death of a child. How often it does so, no one knows—some say it is infrequent, some say it may not be as unusual as we'd like to believe. But the moral question is, how much risk to an innocent child are we willing to take for the sake of convenience? We may come to different conclusions, to be sure, but unless the evidence is laid on the table, people can't bring their own ethical values to bear on these matters involving themselves and their children.

Dr. Goodnough says "It is particularly distressing that Alcorn refers to studies in order to make a point, even though one would be hard pressed to find actual support for the point within the context of the study." If by "support for the point" he means that the authors cited don't state the conclusion "oral contraceptives cause abortions," obviously that is true. I've researched and written sixteen books and many articles. It is standard practice in presenting one's research to selectively cite Plato, C. S. Lewis, *The New York Times*, or *The New England Journal of Medicine*, without implying that they necessarily agree with your particular conclusion. If we limited our citations only to those who have reached the same conclusion as we have, it would prohibit us from presenting evidence for any new or unpopular viewpoint. I present dozens of threads of evidence, documented in 138 endnotes. That some of those cited would not agree with my conclusions or share my ethical concerns is obviously true.

Dr. Goodnough does exactly what I did (indeed, so must every researcher) when he selectively cites certain statements from studies, not one of which states "oral contraceptives cannot cause abortions." I disagree with his conclusions, but I do not find it distressing that he pulls data from sources which make no claim whatsoever to support his conclusions.

Dr. Goodnough admits that many sources, including *The Physician's Desk Reference,* refer to the effects on the endometrium as "reducing the likelihood of implantation." He then calls such statements "speculation." I always find this interesting. The disclosure of the medical information contained in *PDR* is mandated by no less an authority than the FDA. The information presented is more than a marketing ploy or a legal caveat. Anyone convinced that the manufacturers' claims that the Pill sometimes prevents implantation are not truthful statements based on science, but false statements motivated by carelessness or public relations, has the responsibility to take this serious accusation to the oral contraceptive companies (all of whom make this claim), not to mention the FDA. Dr. Goodnough and others should *not* expect either physicians or the general public to simply disregard this medical information from qualified research departments in favor of the more desirable (for prolifers) belief that the Pill really can't do what the pharmaceutical researchers all believe and claim it can.

Dr. Goodnough says, "in light of the fact that there is no definitive information on whether the embryo implants or not, [Randy Alcorn] could just as easily assume that the embryo always implants and survives despite seemingly hostile changes in the endometrium." I would certainly like to make this assumption, as it would relieve me of any sense of moral obligation. Unfortunately, the assumption seems to be based on wishful thinking, not scientific observation or logic. It is clearly *not* equally valid to draw either conclusion after looking at what everyone, even Dr. Goodnough, agrees are "seemingly hostile changes in the endometrium" caused by OCPs. To admit that this appears to be true and then to say—without producing any evidence to support it—that one might just as well conclude the embryo "always implants and survives" is nonsensical, isn't it?

If the endometrium appears to be hostile, clearly the burden of proof falls upon those, such as Dr. Goodnough, who argue it is not (or, who argue that conception and a hostile endometrium are mutually exclusive). Dr. Goodnough needs to produce evidence to show that a *seemingly* hostile endometrium is not a *truly* hostile endometrium. But he fails to do so. In the absence of such evidence, aren't we forced to assume that the endometrium is indeed what it seems to be—hostile (though not absolutely prohibitive) to implantation? To present these conclusions as equally valid, in the absence of evidence supporting what is contradictory to empirical observation, is untenable.

Among those who have no vested interests, I have virtually never found anyone arguing that the Pill cannot or does not hinder implantation. The *only* people I've found who make that assumption are those who have vested interests in doing so—prolifers who use, prescribe or recommend oral contraceptives, but do not (understandably) wish to believe they can jeopardize human life.

My most serious concern with Goodnough's article is a misrepresentation of my argument, followed by a striking misquotation from my book. The misrepresentation is claiming that I "attempt to equate the so-called morning-after pill with the OCP." In fact, I do *not* equate the two—I simply point out that the morning-after-pill is not some novel chemical invention, but four standard OCPs taken together

185

(suggesting that the pills already have something in them which raises the frequency of an abortifacient effect as the dosage increases). But to back up his misrepresentation of my point, Dr. Goodnough quotes me as saying that the morning after pill "increases the chances of doing what it [the birth control pill] already does—cause an abortion."

That does indeed sound like I'm equating the two. Dr. Goodnough follows by expressing dismay that I could say such a thing. When I read the quotation, I too was dismayed. Why? Because I knew what other readers wouldn't—I did *not* say this. What I actually said, in all five editions of the book (Goodnough quotes from the second)—was this: the morning after pill "increases the chances of doing what it [the OCP] already *sometimes* does—cause an abortion."

Dr. Goodnough left out the all-important word "sometimes." This makes it appear I was claiming the OCP, like the morning after pill, acts primarily as an abortifacient. That would be an erroneous claim, of course. Indeed, readers of Dr. Goodnough's article now believe I was making that very claim. Any one who could have read what I actually said would know I was **not**. Unfortunately, this correction will never reach most of those who read the article, and will read it in the future. I am disappointed that such a misquotation was not corrected during the peer-review process of *Ethics and Medicine*. I can only hope Dr. Goodnough did not also leave out similarly critical words when he cited other sources, but I have no assurance this is the case.

I am not straining out gnats here. It is one thing to misunderstand an author and in the process misrepresent his position to others. It is another thing to actually revise what an author has said, in this case leaving out a critical operative word, resulting in misrepresenting the author and misleading the reader. I trust that was not Dr. Goodnough's *intention*, of course. But it certainly was the *result*.

This critical gap between intentions and results leads naturally to my final and most serious concern about Goodnough's theories, one that lies at the heart of my disagreement with him. He says, "When I prescribe the OCP, I do not want an embryo to die. The death of the embryo, should it occur, is the undesired result of intending to prevent fertilization" (p. 45).

First, we should remember that some patients will consider the risk of carrying an unwanted child as less serious than the risk of killing an unwanted child. They will think in terms not simply of the preferences of adults to not have children, but the welfare of children themselves. We certainly all want physicians to have clear consciences—but let's not forget their patients also have consciences, and it is of paramount importance that the patient be able to act in good conscience, informed by their physician of the existing evidence, and the interpretations of not one, but both schools of thought.

But my main concern is with this matter of intentions. As a college ethics professor and author of several books on ethical issues I've interacted with people in hundreds of different vocations. Interestingly, I have found that the logic of "sincerity and good intentions makes something right" seems more prevalent among medical professionals than any other group.

I certainly agree most women taking the Pill don't intend to get abortions. In fact, I'm convinced 99% of them are unaware this is even possible. (This is precisely the problem, and why we need true informed consent by Pill-takers.)

The fact remains that while the *intentions* of those taking the Pill may be harmless, the *results* can be every bit as fatal. A nurse giving a child an injection may sincerely intend no harm to a child. But if she mistakenly injects him with a fatal poison, her good intentions will in no way lessen the tragedy. Whether the nurse has the heart of a murderer or a saint, the child is equally dead. The best intentions do nothing to reverse the most disastrous results.

Even if the Pill doesn't usually cause an abortion, whenever it *does* do so it is just as real an abortion as if that were its intended effect. So, I certainly believe that when he prescribes OCPs, Dr. Goodnough does not want an embryo to die. But I find that irrelevant to the question at hand. The chances of the embryo's (I prefer the term "pre-born child's") death is in no way lessened by the prescribing physician's or the mother's or anyone else's intentions.

By all means, let us be sincere and intend only to do good. But we must never argue for the legitimacy of a course of action based on our sincerity and good intentions. We must act instead in light of the actual evidence that indicates what consequences may come from the action itself. Whether or not an action is moral depends on a number of factors, not least of which is the possible impact on the welfare of a human being. This is particularly true when it involves an innocent human being who is unable to speak up for himself, and for whom we are commanded by God to act as advocates (Proverbs 31:8-9).

Endnotes:

[1] "The Impact of the Pill on Implantation Factors—New Research Findings," *Ethics & Medicine 2000*, vol. 16.1, 15-22.

[2] John F. Kilner, *The Reproduction Revolution: A Christian Appraisal of Sexuality, Reproductive Technologies, and the Family,* Dr. Walter Larimore and Randy Alcorn, "Using the Birth Control Pill Is Ethically Unacceptable," (Grand Rapids, Eerdmans, 2000), 179-191.

[3] Eugene F. Diamond, "Word Wars: Games People Play about the Beginning of Life," *Physician,* November/December 1992, 14-15. For more on this also see DA Grimes, RJ Cook, "Mifepristone (RU-486)—an abortifacient to prevent abortion?" *New England Journal of Medicine*, 1992;327:1088-9 and DA Grimes, "Emergency contraception—expanding opportunities for primary prevention," *New England Journal of Medicine*," 1997;337:1078-9.

[4] Randy C. Alcorn, *ProLife Answers to ProChoice Arguments*, (Multnomah Press, 1992, 1994), 118.

[5] *Danforth's Obstetrics and Gynecology,* 7th edition, (Philadelphia: J. B. Lippincott Co., 1994), 626.

[6] Nine Van der Vange, "Ovarian activity during low dose oral contraceptives," *Contemporary Obstetrics and Gynecology*, edited by G. Chamberlain (London: Butterworths, 1988), 315-16.

[7] Advertisement by the Association of Reproductive Health Professionals and Ortho Pharmaceutical Corporation, *Hippocrates*, May/June 1988, 35.

[8] Pharmacists for Life, *Oral Contraceptives and IUDs: Birth Control or Abortifacients?,* November 1989, 1.

[9] The Physician's Desk Reference, 1995, 1775.

[10] Ibid, 1782.

[11] Ibid, 2461.

[12] Ibid, 2685.

[13] Ibid, 2693.

[14] Ibid, 2743.

[15] Ibid, 1744.

[16] Package insert dated July 12, 1994, Demulen, manufactured by Searle.

[17] John F. Kilner, *The Reproduction Revolution: A Christian Appraisal of Sexuality, Reproductive Technologies, and the Family,* Dr. Walter Larimore and Randy Alcorn, "Using the Birth Control Pill Is Ethically Unacceptable," (Grand Rapids, Eerdmans, 2000), 179-191.

[18] Ibid, Dr. Susan Crockett, et. al., "Using Hormone Contraceptives Is a Decision Involving Science, Scripture, and Conscience," 192-201.

[19] Ibid, 193.

[20] Ibid, Walter Larimore and Randy Alcorn, 180.

[21] Brian Clowes, Ph.D., Fact Sheet—*Contraceptive Pills Abortifacient,* www.hli.org/issues/contraception/other/pillsabort.html.

[22] Stephen G. Somkuti, et al., "The effect of oral contraceptive pills on markers of endometrial receptivity," *Fertility and Sterility*, Volume 65, #3, March 1996, 488.

[23] Shoham, Z., Di Carlo, C., Patel, A., *et al.,* "Is it possible to Run a Successful Ovulation Induction Based Solely on Ultrasound Monitoring? The Importance of Endometrial Measurements," *Fert. Steril.*, (1991); 56, 5, 836-41.

[24] Drs. Chowdhury, Joshi and Associates, "Escape ovulation in women due to the missing of low dose combination oral contraceptive pills," *Contraception*, September 1980, 241.

[25] "The Phasic Approach to Oral Contraception," *The International Journal of Fertility*, volume 28, 1988, 129.

[26] Dr. Goldzieher, *Hormonal Contraception*, 122.

[27] Cunningham, et al, *Williams Obstetrics* (Stamford, CT: Appleton & Lange, 1993), 1323.

[28] Drs. Ulstein and Myklebust, "Ultrastructure of Cervical Mucus and Sperm Penetration During Use of a Triphasic Oral Contraceptive," *Acta Obstet Gynecol Scand Suppl,* 1982) 105.

[29] *Drug Facts and Comparisons,* 1996 edition.

[30] *Danforth's Obstetrics and Gynecology* (Philadelphia: J. B. Lippincott Co., 1994, 7th edition) 626.

[31] Potter, "How Effective Are Contraceptives? The determination and measurement of pregnancy rates," *Obstetrics and Gynecology* 1996, 135:13S-23S.

[32] Drs. Walter Larimore and Joseph Stanford, "Postfertilization effects of oral contraceptives and their relation to informed consent," *Archives of Family Medicine* 2000;9:133.

http://archfami.ama-assn.org/issues/v9n2/rfull/fac9006.html.

[33] Dr. Chris Kahlenborn, "How the pill and other contraceptives work; Can a Christian take the Pill?" *Life Advocate*, 1997;12(7).

[34] Sherrill Sellman, "A Bitter Pill to Swallow," *Nexus*, June-July 1997, 27.

[35] Dr. Kristine Severyn, "Abortifacient Drugs and Devices: Medical and Moral Dilemmas," *Linacre Quarterly*, August 1990, 55.

[36] Cohen, S.A., "Objections, Confusion Among Pharmacists Threaten Access to Emergency Contraception," *The Guttmacher Report on Public Health, June 1999, 1-3*.

[37] Robert Hatcher, *et al.*, *Contraceptive Technology,* 16th Revised Edition, Irvington Publishers, New York, 1994, 224.

[38] Yoshimura, Y., "Integrins: Expression, Modulation, and Signaling in Fertilization, Embryo genesis and Implantation," *Keio Journal of Medicine*, 1997; 46(1), 17, 20.

[39] The Couple to Couple League, "The Pill: How does it work? Is it safe?" (Cincinnati, OH), 4.

[40] Dr. Alan Guttmacher, "Prevention of Conception Through Contraception and Sterilization," *Gynecology and Obstetrics*, Vol.1, C. H. Davis, ed. (Baltimore: Williams and Wilkins, 1966), 8.

[41] Dr. Daniel R. Mishell, "Current Status of Oral Contraceptive Steroids, *Clinical Obstetrics & Gynecology* 19:4, December 1976, 746.

[42] Dr. J. Richard Crout, *FDA Consumer*, HEW publication number 76-3024, reprinted from May, 1976.

[43] J. Peel and M. Potts, *Textbook of Contraceptive Practice* (Cambridge University Press), 8.

[44] P. G. Crosignani and D. R. Mishell, *Ovulation In the Human*, (Academic Press, Inc., 1976), 150.

[45] *Handbook of Obstetrics & Gynecology*, (6th edition, 1977), 689-690.

[46] Ortho Pharmaceutical Corporation, *A Guide to Methods of Contraception*, (Raritan, NJ: Ortho, 1979), 8.

[47] "What We Know About the Pill," *Changing Times*, July 1977, 21.

191

[48] Stewart, Guess, Stewart, Hatcher, *My Body, My Health*, Clinician's Edition (Wiley Medical Publications, 1979), 169-70.

[49] Ruth Colker, *The Dallas Morning News*, February 6, 1992, 23A.

[50] Frank Sussman, representing Missouri Abortion Clinics, New York Times, National Edition, April 27, 1989, 15 & B13.

[51] www.nau.edu/~fronske/bcp.html

[52] Dr. Stephen Killick, *Fertility and Sterility*, October 1989, 580

[53] Dr. David Sterns, *"How the Pill and the IUD Work: Gambling with Life"* (American Life League, Stamford, VA 22555).

[54] Ibid.

[55] Dr. Nine Van der Vange, "Ovarian activity during low dose oral contraceptives," *Contemporary Obstetrics and Gynecology*, edited by G. Chamberlain (London: Butterworths, 1988), 323-24.

[56] John Wilks, "The Impact of the Pill on Implantation Factors— New Research Findings," 19.

[57] Joel E. Goodnough, "Redux: Is the Oral Contraceptive Pill an Abortifacient," *Ethics & Medicine,* p. 39, vol. 17:1, Spring 2001.

[58] Barbara Struthers, Searle's Director of Healthcare Information Services, a letter dated February 13, 1997.

[59] Dr. G. Virginia Upton, "The Phasic Approach to Oral Contraception," *The International Journal of Fertility,* vol. 28, 1988, 129.

[60] William Colliton, Jr., *Birth Control Pill: Abortifacient and Contraceptive, Linacre Quarterly,* November 1999, 31, from the American Association of Prolife Obstetricians and Gynecologists (AAPLOG), mid-winter session, 1998.

[61] Manual produced by Wyeth-Ayerst, "Oral Contraceptive Backgrounder."

[62] Karen Witt, Sales Representative for Whitehall-Robins, sister company of Wyeth-Ayerst, Interview on July 2, 1997.

[63] The respective rates of increase in the five studies are 70%, 80%, 330%, 350% and 1390%. The studies, cited by Dr. Larimore in his email, are as follows: (1) "A multinational case-control study of ectopic pregnancy," *Clin Reprod Fertil* 1985;3:131-143; (2) Mol BWJ, Ankum WM, Bossuyt PMM, and Van der Veen F, "Contraception and the risk of ectopic pregnancy: a meta analysis," *Contraception* 1995;52:337-341; (3) Job-Spira N, Fernandez H, Coste J,

Papiernik E, Spira A, "Risk of Chlamydia PID and oral contraceptives," *J Am Med Assoc* 1990;264:2072-4; (4) Thorburn J, Berntsson C, Philipson M, Lindbolm B, "Background factors of ectopic pregnancy: Frequency distribution in a case-control study," *Eur J Obstet Gynecol Reprod Biol* 1986;23:321-331; (5) Coste J, Job-Spira N, Fernandez H, Papiernik E, Spira A, "Risk factors for ectopic pregnancy: a case-control study in France, with special focus on infectious factors," *Am J Epidemiol* 1991;133:839-49.

[64] Walter Larimore, "Ectopic Pregnancy with Oral Contraceptive Use has been Overlooked" (Letters), *British Medical Journal;* 321:1450, August 12, 2000.

[65] Leon Speroff and Philip Darney, *A Clinical Guide for Contraception* (Williams & Wilkins, 1992), 40.

[66] Dr. Paul Hayes, E-mail dated February 22, 1997.

[67] Larry Frieders, in Denny Hartford, "The New Abortionists," *Life Advocate*, March 1994, 26.

[68] Dr. Thomas Hilgers, in "The New Abortionists," *Life Advocate,* March 1994, 28-29.

[69] e.g. Stephen G. Somkuti, et al., "The effect of oral contraceptive pills on markers of endometrial receptivity," *Fertility and Sterility*, Volume 65, #3, March 1996, 484-88; Chowdhury and Joshi, "Escape Ovulation in Women Due to the Missing of Low Dose Combination Oral Contraceptive Pills," *Contraception*, September 1980, 241-247.

[70] Stewart, Guess, Stewart, Hatcher, My Body, *My Health*, Clinician's Edition, (Wiley Medical Publications, 1979), 169-70.

[71] "Facts About Oral Contraceptives," U.S. Department of Health and Human Services, 1984.

[72] "Pregnancy Due to Pill Failure," Package insert for Desogen which is produced by Organon.

[73] Nicholas Tonti-Rilippini, "The Pill: Abortifacient or Contraceptive? A Literature Review," *Linacre Quarterly*, February 1995, 8-9.

[74] "FDA panel: Birth control pills safe as morning after drug," *The Virginian-Pilot*, June 29, 1996, A1, A6.

[75] Peter Modica, "FDA Nod to 'Morning-After' Pill Is Lauded," *Medical Tribune News Service*, February 26, 1997.

[76] Ibid.

[77] *World*, March 8, 1997, 9.

[78] ACOG News Release, "Pharmacists Limit Women's Access to Emergency Contraception," May 18, 1999, www.acog.com/from_home/publications/press_releases/Nr0599ec.htm

[79] Marilyn Elias, "Docs spread word: Pill works on morning after," *USA Today,* April 29, 1997, 1A.

[80] David B. Brushwood, *American Journal of Hospital Pharmacy*, February 1990, vol. 47, 396.

[81] Dr. Christie, "Advances in Oral Contraception," *The Journal of Reproductive Medicine,* January 1983, 100 ff.

[82] Ibid.

[83] Potter, "How Effective Are Contraceptives? The determination and measurement of pregnancy rates," *Obstetrics and Gynecology* 1996, 135:13S-23S.

[84] *Today's Christian Woman*, July/August 1995, 64-65.

[85] Ibid.

[86] Dr. Mastroianni, title and date unknown, photocopied article.

[87] Wm Colliton, Jr., "Birth Control Pill: Abortifacient or Contraceptive?" *LinacreQuarterly,* November, 1999, 31.

[88] Ibid., 29.

[89] Sheldon J. Segal, et. al, "Norplant implants: the mechanism of contraceptive action," *Fertility and Sterility*, 1991, 274-277.

[90] A collaborative effort by several very active pro-life OB-GYN specialists screened through about twenty additional OB-GYN specialists, "Birth Control Pills: Contraceptive or Abortifacient?" E-mail sent January 30, 1998.

[91] Ibid.

[92] Ibid.

[93] Ibid.

[94] Wm Colliton, Jr., "Birth Control Pill: Abortifacient or Contraceptive?" *LinacreQuarterly,* November, 1999, 26.

[95] Ibid., 35.

[96] Dr. Harry Kraus, E-mail dated December 23, 1996.

[97] Dr. Rudolph Ehmann , *Abortifacient Contraception: The Pharmaceutical Holocaust* (Human Life International, 1993) 7.

[98] Dr. Bogomir M. Kuhar, *Infant Homicides Through Contraceptives,* 26.

[99] Dr. Thomas Hilgers, "The New Abortionists," *Life Advocate*, March 1994, 29.

[100] Dr. Nine van der Vange, At the Society for the Advancement of Contraception's November 26-30, 1984, conference in Jakarta.

[101] H. Kuhl, et. al, "A Randomized Cross-over Comparison of Two Low-Dose Oral Contraceptives," *Contraception*, June 1985, 583.

[102] Chowdhury and Joshi, "Escape Ovulation in Women Due to the Missing of Low Dose Combination Oral Contraceptive Pills," *Contraception*, September 1980, 241-247.

[103] J. C. Espinoza, M.D., *Birth Control: Why Are They Lying to Women?*, 28.

[104] Dr. Jack Willke, *Abortion Question and Answers*, published online by Ohio Right to Life.

[105] Dr. Kuhar, *Contraceptives can Kill Babies*, American Life League, 1994, 1.

[106] Drs. Chang & Hunt, "Effects of various progestins and estrogen on the gamete transport and fertilization in the rabbit," *Fertility and Sterility*, 1970, 21, 683-686.

[107] Dr. Melvin Taymor, Harvard Medical School, "Some thoughts on the postcoital test," *Fertility and Sterility*, November 1988, 702.

[108] Michael J. Zinaman, "Estimates of human fertility and pregnancy loss," *Fertility and Sterility*, March 1996, 503.

[109] Dr. Bogomir Kuhar, *Infant Homicides Through Contraceptives*, 27.

[110] Dr. David Sterns, "*How the Pill and the IUD Work: Gambling with Life*," American Life League, Stafford, VA.

[111] Dr. T. B. Woutersz, "A Low-Dose Combination Oral Contraceptive," *The Journal of Reproductive Medicine*, December 1981, 620.

[112] Dr. James Trussel, *Pediatric News*, Letters to the Editor, October 1997.

[113] Oz Hopkins Koglin, "Washington leads test of 'morning after' pills," *The Oregonian*, February 26, 1998, A1.

[114] Debra Evans, An appendix in *The Woman's Complete Guide to Personal Health Care*, (Wolgemuth & Hyatt Publishers, 1991), 319-322.

[115] Dr. James Walker, "*Oral Contraception: A Different Perspective*," Pharmacists for Life, PO Box 1281, Powell, OH, 43065.

[116] Dr. Paul Hayes, E-mail dated August 15, 1997.

[117] Dr. Walter L. Larimore, "The Growing Debate About the Abortifacient Effect of the Birth Control Pill and the Principle of Double Effect," *Ethics & Medicine* Journal, January 2000;16(1):23-30). Also available in an updated format at www.epm.org/pilldebate.html

[118] Ibid, www.epm.org/pilldebate.html

[119] Dr. Leon Speroff, *Clinical Gynecologic Endocrinology and Infertility* (Williams and Wilkins, 5th edition, 1994), 937-39.

[120] Drs. Kline, Stein & Susser, *Conception to Birth*, (New York: Oxford University Press, 1989), 54-55.

[121] Michael J. Zinaman, et. al., *Fertility and Sterility*, March 1996, 503-504.

[122] *Natural Family Planning: Safe, Healthy, Effective*, Cincinnati, OH, 1.

[123] E-mail from a Christian physician who is also a Marriage and Family Therapist.

[124] Dr. Walter Larimore, E-mail dated February 26, 1998.

[125] John F. Kilner, *The Reproduction Revolution: A Christian Appraisal of Sexuality, Reproductive Technologies, and the Family, pp. 193, .* Dr. Susan Crockett, et. al., "Using Hormone Contraceptives Is a Decision Involving Science, Scripture, and Conscience," Eerdmans Publ., Grand Rapids, 2000.

[126] Christian Medical & Dental Association Position Statement, www.epm.org/CMDAstate.html

[127] T.L. Beauchamp, "Informed Consent," in *Medical Ethics*, ed. R.M. Veatch, (Boston: Jones & Bartlett, 1989), 173-200.

[128] David Biebel, "Professional Suicide or Personal Surrender?" *Today's Christian Doctor*, March 1, 1998, www.cmds.org/index.cgi?cat=151&art=692&BISKIT=729669149&CONTEXT=art

[129] N. Wagner, "K-Mart pharmacist refuses to fill prescriptions for 'morning after' pill, *The Salt Lake Tribune*, June 5 1997, B1, B4.

[130] Information on the Pharmacist's Conscience Clause is available at Pharmacists for Life's website at www.pfli.org

[131] Robert Hatcher, *et al.*, *Contraceptive Technology*, 16th Revised Edition, Irvington Publishers, New York, 1994, Dedication.

[132] Kaiser Family Foundation, 1995 Survey of Obstetrician/Gynecologists on Conception and Unplanned

Pregnancy: Attitude and Practices with regard to Abortion, Menlo Park, California; cited by Lawrence Roberge, "The Future of Abortion," *Life Advocate*, March 1997, 30.

[133] Irving Sivin , "IUDs are Contraceptives, Not Abortifacients: A Comment on Research and Belief," *Studies in Family Planning*, Vol. 20, Number 6, November-December 1989, 355-59.

[134] Dr. Eugene Diamond, "RU-486—the rest of the story," *Family Resources Center News,* January 1993, Peoria, Illinois. Also found at www.vitalsignsministries.org/vsmru486.html

[135] *Drug Facts & Comparisons*, 1996 edition, 419.

[136] R. W. Kistner, *Gynecology: Principles & Practices* (YearBook Medical Publishers, 3rd edition, 1979), 735.

[137] Dr. Joseph W. Goldzieher, *Hormonal Contraception: Pills, Injections & Implants,* (Essential Medical Information Systems, PO Box 811247, Dallas, Texas), 35.

[138] Searle leaflet, 1981.

[139] *The Physician's Desk Reference*, 1996 edition, 1872.